First World War Poetry

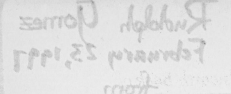

The Wordsworth Book of
First World War Poetry

*Selected, with an Introduction
and Bibliography, by Marcus Clapham*

They shall grow not old, as we that are left grow old:
Age shall not weary them, nor the years condemn.
At the going down of the sun and in the morning
We will remember them.

LAURENCE BINYON

Wordsworth Poetry Library

This edition published 1995 by Wordsworth Editions Ltd,
Cumberland House, Crib Street, Ware, Hertfordshire SG12 9ET.

ISBN 1-85326-444-X

Typeset in the UK by Antony Gray.
Printed and bound in Denmark by Nørhaven.

INTRODUCTION

Memorials to the Great War abound, from the grand, such as the New Menin Gate in Belgium and Lutyens's Cenotaph in Whitehall, London, to the neat and beautifully tended military cemeteries which stretch from the North Sea to the Swiss border, as well as the countless stone crosses in villages and churches across Europe. However, it is perhaps the poetry to which that war gave birth which is the most poignant legacy and which will be the most enduring memorial to the millions of dead and wounded in that monstrous act of folly. The Great War was senseless; senseless in its outbreak, senseless in its prosecution, senseless in the slaughter of what became a lost generation. Perhaps the fascination of that conflict lies less in a morbid interest in the mud and carnage than in the fact that it marks a caesura in the development of modern history. It changed the social, political and military orders in a way that no previous war – with the possible exception of the American Civil War – had done before.

In 1914, the British, Austrian and French empires were at their apogee, and Germany, under the Hohenzollerns, was rapidly becoming the foremost economic power in Europe. Russia was a sleeping giant, the Turkish empire was collapsing from internal and external pressure, and the Balkans were – the Balkans. The affluence of the European middle classes enabled them to travel for both pleasure and education, and in many ways Europe was more cosmopolitan then than it is now. And yet *ennui* was prevalent among the educated young bourgeois, who had no new worlds to conquer, and who saw ahead of them an almost endless wait for influence as the elder generations clung on to their power. In spite of the three great European empires and Germany's struggle for its 'place in the sun', many of the young men were 'ardent for some desperate glory'. When war broke out in August 1914, it was

welcomed as high adventure, a sort of military football match that
would be over by Christmas.

> Now, God be thanked . . .

wrote Rupert Brooke

> . . . Who has matched us with His hour,
> And caught our youth, and wakened us from sleeping.

Even Siegfried Sassoon, later the most savage of the trench poets,
welcomed the news of war, and enlisted at once in the Sussex
Yeomanry, taking with him his beloved hunter, Cockbird.

At the outbreak of war, the mainstream of English poetry was
greatly influenced by Harold Monro's Poetry Bookshop, from
which he published Sir Edward Marsh's anthologies, *Georgian
Poetry*. The circle of Georgian poets included Rupert Brooke, John
Drinkwater and Lascelles Abercrombie, and Sassoon, Edmund
Blunden and Isaac Rosenberg were also intimates. Georgian poetry
was largely pastoral and romantic, and could therefore be used to
convey the optimistic and chivalrous feelings of the first heady
months of the war. But the mood did not survive long. Within six
months the war had settled into the near-stalemate of trench
warfare on the Western Front, and at Ypres in April 1915, the
Germans used poison gas for the first time.

The muddle and the waste could no longer be disguised from
the fighting soldier, and Julian Grenfell was moved to write his
mildly satirical 'Prayer for Those on the Staff'. But two months
later, his famous 'Into Battle' still shows the pervading influence of
the Georgian poets, and it was not until October of 1915 that the
voice of the soldier-poet came to be expressed accurately in
Charles Sorley's last poem, 'When you see millions of the mouthless
dead'. Disillusion with the High Command and the Home Front
had set in.

Any remaining niceties of poetry were shattered by the guns
which opened the Battle of the Somme on 1st July 1916. Kitchener's
New Armies, together with the remains of the Old Contemptibles
and more recent volunteers were committed to 'The Big Push'. On
the first day alone there were nearly 60,000 casualties, one-third of
them fatal. Romantic and pastoral verse could not convey the
horror of this battle which lasted four months. In August, Sassoon
was invalided home with trench fever, and found his voice in the

bitter poems 'They' and 'Blighters'. Sassoon never lost the anger to be found in these poems and from 1916 to 1927 his scathing poetry stung the conscience of his readers.

Sassoon was a man of physical and moral courage. He was awarded the Military Cross (he subsequently threw the decoration ribbon into the Mersey in disgust) in June 1916, was wounded in April 1917 and sent home again. While convalescing, he came to the reasonable conclusion that the continuation of the war was not for liberty but for commercial and territorial aggrandisement. With the encouragement of like-minded people, including Bertrand Russell, he prepared a statement setting out his views, which he sent to his Colonel. (It was subsequently read out in the House of Commons and reprinted in *The Times*.) In a manner worthy of 1984 or the Soviet Union at its nastiest, it was decided that Sassoon was indeed the 'Mad Jack' of his regimental nickname, and he was sent to Craiglockhart Psychiatric Hospital in Edinburgh. There, he met the shell-shocked Wilfred Owen. Sassoon's sympathy and encouragement enabled Owen to give expression to his poetic concern – the pity of war.

Sassoon and Owen are the two giants of the English poets of the First World War. Sassoon's poetry expressed the fierce anger of the poet, as a fighting man. It was unfamiliar and unpopular at the time because war poetry had rarely been written by an active participant. Owen, on the other hand, moved beyond the anger to a deep compassion, which the public was more ready to receive after the war, when Owen's poetry was published posthumously.

Sassoon and Owen were by no means the only poets. Blunden, Rosenberg and Robert Graves were writing and corresponding vigorously. Major and interesting poems of the First World War emerge from unexpected places. There are those by acknowledged poets like Thomas Hardy, whose 'Channel Firing' of 1912 reads as an eerie prophecy of things to come. Henry Newbolt's 'The Vigil' and 'A Letter from the Front' show how out of touch was that imperialist poetaster, and the bitterness of Rudyard Kipling's poetry after the death of his son John at the Battle of Loos in 1915 contrasts sharply with his earlier work, such as *Barrack Room Ballads*. It was not simply officers and established poets who contributed to the canon of First World War poetry. Rosenberg remained a private throughout his service; Manning, Saki and Thomas all refused commissions, and Gurney, Macdonald, Coulson and Streets never rose above non-commissioned rank; and the anonymous songs and poems express the feelings of the other ranks. The deep emotion, revulsion – and humour – were not just the province of the educated.

After the end of 'the war to end all wars', the poetry that it engendered was not fashionable. W. B. Yeats believed, with others, that 'passive suffering was not a fit subject for poetry'. The poets themselves – those who survived – found that the 'land fit for heroes' lived only in the rhetoric of politicians. As early as 1916, Philip Johnstone's 'High Wood' anticipates the indifference of a conducted tour as it visits a battlefield. Sassoon's 'On Passing the New Menin Gate' –

> Who will remember, passing through this Gate,
> The unheroic Dead who fed the guns?

is an anguished cry for those whose sacrifice seemed vain. Yet, eighty years after the First World War, it is, perhaps, because of Sassoon and his fellow poets that we *do* remember. Those visiting the New Menin Gate in Ypres today will be moved, in a way that Sassoon could not be, by the ceremony at sunset each night when four *sapeurs-pompiers* play the 'Last Post' beneath it.

In making this selection, an attempt has been made to draw as widely as possible from the poets who actually fought. There are, necessarily, many omissions. Robert Graves was not keen to have his war poetry anthologised; poets such as Herbert Read and A. P. Herbert are better known for their other writing. It is arguable that Edmund Blunden is under-represented; it is equally arguable that his feelings are better expressed in his autobiographical *Undertones of War*. The arrangement is equally arbitrary. To arrange it by date of composition is impossible, since the date is unknown in many cases. Arrangement by date of death of the poet is as unsatisfactory for obvious reasons, and a thematic organisation raises as many questions as it answers. So, an alphabetical structure is used for ease of reference.

The Wordsworth Book of First World War Poetry is intended as an introduction to the poetry which has had so great an influence on the development of English poetry. Other anthologies, listed below, shed similar, but different, light. Also listed are some of the more important prose works.

Marcus Clapham
London, 1995

FURTHER READING

Poetry Anthologies

Gardner, Brian (ed.), *Up the Line to Death*, Methuen, 1964

Parsons, I. M. (ed.), *Men Who March Away*, Chatto & Windus, 1965

Powell, Anne (ed.), *A Deep Cry*, Palladour Books, 1993

Silkin, Jon (ed.), *The Penguin Book of First World War Poetry*, 2nd edition 1981

Stallworthy, Jon, *The Oxford Book of War Poetry*, Oxford University Press, 1984

Stephen, Martin (ed.), *Never Such Innocence*, Buchan & Enright, 1988

Walsh, Colin (ed.), *Mud, Songs & Blighty: A Scrapbook of the First World War*, Hutchinson, 1975

Prose Works

Blunden, Edmund, *Undertones of War*, 1928

Graves, Robert, *Goodbye to All That*, 1929

Herbert, A. P., *The Secret Battle*, 1919

Manning, Frederic, *Her Privates We*, 1930

Sassoon, Siegfried, *Memoirs of an Infantry Officer*, 1930

Sassoon, Siegfried, *Sherston's Progress*, 1936

Stallworthy, Jon, *Wilfred Owen*, 1974

ACKNOWLEDGEMENTS

For permission to reprint copyright material, the publishers gratefully acknowledge the following:

Rosica Colin Ltd for 'Bombardment' © The Estate of Richard Aldington
Aitken, Stone & Wylie Ltd for 'The Deserter' by Gilbert Frankau
Carcanet Press Ltd for 'The Zonnebeke Road', '1916 Seen from 1921' and 'Two Voices' by Edmund Blunden, and 'A Soldier Addresses His Body' and 'Winter Warfare' by Edgell Rickword
George Sassoon for 'The Death-Bed', 'They', 'Base Details', 'The General', 'Dreamers', 'A Working Party', 'Wirers', 'Attack', 'Counter-Attack', 'The Rearguard', 'Glory of Women', 'Does It Matter?', 'Suicide in the Trenches', 'Memorial Tablet', 'Aftermath' and 'On Passing the New Menin Gate' by Siegfried Sassoon

In this anthology, the publishers have made every effort to trace the copyright holders of all the poems still in copyright. They would be interested to hear from any copyright holders not here acknowledged.

For their help and advice, the editor would like to extend his warmest thanks to Donald McFarlan and Clive Reynard.

CONTENTS

LIST OF CONTRIBUTORS

Aldington, Richard 1892–1962

Beckh, Robert Harold 1894–1916. Killed, Arras, 14th August

Berridge, William Eric 1894–1916. Died of wounds, Delville
    Wood, 20th August

Bishop, John Peale 1892–1944

Blunden, Edmund 1896–1974

Bridges, Robert 1844–1930

Brooke, Rupert 1887–1915. Died, Greece, 21st April

Chesterton, Gilbert Keith 1874–1936

Coulson, Leslie 1889–1916. Died of wounds, the Somme,
    8th October

Ford, Ford Madox 1873–1939

Frankau, Gilbert 1884–1952

Freeman, John 1880–1929

Galsworthy, John 1867–1933

Grenfell, Julian Henry Francis 1888–1915. Died of wounds,
    Boulogne, 26th May

Gurney, Ivor Bertie 1890–1937

Hardy, Thomas 1840–1928

Hodgson, William Noel 1893–1916. Killed, the Somme, 1st July

Housman, Alfred Edward 1859–1936

Hulme, Thomas Ernest 1883–1917. Killed, Belgium,
    28th September

Johnstone, Philip; 'High Wood' was first published in *The Nation*,
    16th February 1918

Kipling, Rudyard 1865–1936

Lyon, Walter Scott Stuart 1893–1915. Killed, Ypres, 8th May

McCrae, John 1872–1918

Mackintosh, Ewart Alan 1893–1917. Killed, Cambrai,
    21st November

Mann, Arthur James (Hamish) 1896–1917. Died of wounds,
    Arras, 10th April

Manning, Frederic 1882–1935

Munro, Neil 1864–1930

Newbolt, Henry John 1862–1938

Nicholls, Robert 1893–1944

Owen, Wilfred Edward Salter 1893–1918. Killed, Sambre Canal,
    4th November

Rickword, John Edgell 1898–1982

Rosenberg, Isaac 1890–1918. Killed, Arras, 1st April

Saki (Hector Hugh Munro) 1870–1916. Killed, the Somme,
    14th November

Sassoon, Siegfried 1886–1967

Seeger, Alan 1888–1916. Killed, the Somme, 4th July

Shaw-Stewart, Patrick Houston 1888–1917. Killed, Cambrai,
    30th December

Smith, Geoffrey Bache 1894–1916. Died of wounds, Arras,
    3rd December

Sorley, Charles Hamilton 1895–1915. Killed, Loos, 13th October

Stewart, John Ebenezer 1889–1918. Killed, Ypres, 26th April

Streets, John William 1885–1916. Killed, the Somme, 1st July

Thomas, Philip Edward 1878–1917. Killed, Arras, 9th April

West, Arthur Graeme 1891–1917. Killed, the Somme, 3rd April

Wilson, Theodore Percival Cameron 1889–1918. Killed, the
    Somme, 23rd March

Yeats, William Butler 1865–1939

RICHARD ALDINGTON
1892–1962

Bombardment

Four days the earth was rent and torn
By bursting steel,
The houses fell about us;
Three nights we dared not sleep,
Sweating, and listening for the imminent crash
Which meant our death.

The fourth night every man,
Nerve-tortured, racked to exhaustion,
Slept, muttering and twitching,
While the shells crashed overhead.

The fifth day there came a hush;
We left our holes
And looked above the wreckage of the earth
To where the white clouds moved in silent lines
Across the untroubled blue.

ANONYMOUS

When this bloody war is over

To the tune of 'What a Friend I have in Jesus'

When this bloody war is over,
Oh, how happy I shall be!
When I get my civvy clothes on
No more soldiering for me.
No more church parades on Sunday,
No more asking for a pass.
I shall tell the Sergeant-Major
To stick his passes up his arse.

When this bloody war is over,
Oh, how happy I shall be.
When I get my civvy clothes on,
No more soldiering for me.
I shall sound my own revally,
I shall make my own tattoo.
No more N.C.O.s to curse me,
No more bleeding Army stew.

N.C.O.s will all be navvies,
Privates ride in motor cars.
N.C.O.s will smoke their Woodbines,
Privates puff their big cigars.
No more standing-to in trenches,
Only one more church parade.
No more shivering on the firestep,
No more Tickler's marmalade.

I don't want to be a soldier

To the tune of 'On Sunday I walk out with a Soldier'

> I don't want to be a soldier,
> I don't want to go to war.
> I'd rather stay at home,
> Around the streets to roam,
> And live on the earnings of a well-paid whore.
> I don't want a bayonet up my arse-hole,
> I don't want my ballocks shot away.
> I'd rather stay in England,
> In merry merry England,
> And fornicate my bloody life away.

Sentry! What of the night?

> Sentry! What of the night?
> The sentry's answer I will not repeat,
> Though short in words 'twas with feeling replete.
> It covered all he thought and more,
> It covered all he'd thought before,
> It covered all he might think yet
> In years to come,
> For he was wet and had no rum.

If you want to find the Sergeant

If you want to find the Sergeant,
I know where he is, I know where he is,
   I know where *he* is.
If you want to find the Sergeant
   I know where he is –
He's lying on the Canteen floor.
I've seen him, I've *seen* him,
Lying on the Canteen floor.

      *   *   *

If you want to find the old battalion,
I know where they are, I know where they are,
   I know where *they* are.
If you want to find the old battalion,
   I know where they are –
They're hanging on the old barbed wire.
I've seen 'em, I've *seen* 'em,
Hanging on the old barbed wire.

R. H. BECKH

1894–1916. Killed, Arras, 14th August

No Man's Land

Nine-Thirty o'clock? Then over the top,
And mind to keep down when you see the flare
Of Very pistol searching the air.
Now, over you get; look out for the wire
In the borrow pit, and the empty tins,
They are meant for the Hun to bark his shins.
So keep well down and reserve your fire –
All over? Right: there's a gap just here
In the corkscrew wire, so just follow me;
If you keep well down there's nothing to fear

*   *   *

Then out we creep thro' the gathering gloom
Of No MAN'S LAND, while the big guns boom
Right over our heads, and the rapid crack
Of the Lewis guns is answered back
By the German barking the same refrain
Of crack, crack, crack, all over again.

To the wistful eye from the parapet,
In the smiling sun of a summer's day,
'Twere a sin to believe that a bloody death
In those waving grasses lurking lay.
But now, 'neath the Very's fitful flares
'Keep still, my lads, and freeze like hares; –
All right, carry on, for we're out to enquire
If our friend the Hun's got a gap in his wire;
And he hasn't invited us out, you see,
So lift up your feet and follow me.'

*   *   *

Then, silent, we press with a noiseless tread
Thro' no man's land, but the sightless dead;
Aye, muffle your footsteps, well ye may,
For the mouldering corpses here decay
Whom no man owns but the King abhorred.
Grim Pluto, Stygia's over-lord.
Oh breathe a prayer for the sightless Dead
Who have bitten the dust 'neath the biting lead
Of the pitiless hail of the Maxim's fire,
'Neath the wash of shell in the well trod mire.
Ah well! But we've, too, got a job to be done,
For we've come to the wire of our friend, the Hun.
'Now, keep well down, lads; can you see any gap?

*   *   *

Not much, well the reference is wrong in the map'
So homeward we go thro' the friendly night.
That covers the No Man's Land from sight,
As muttering a noiseless prayer of praise,
We drop from the parapet into the bays.

WILLIAM ERIC BERRIDGE

1894–1916

Died of wounds, Delville Wood, 20th August

To a Rat

Caught on a piece of wire in a
communication trench 4.45 a.m. April 1916

Was it for this you came into the light?
Have you fulfilled Life's mission? You are free
For evermore from toil and misery,
Yet those who snared you, to their great delight,
Thought doubtless they were only doing right
In scheming to encompass your decease,
Forgetting they were bringing you to peace
And perfect joy and everlasting night.
Your course is ended here – I know not why
You seemed a loathsome, a pernicious creature;
You couldn't clothe us and we couldn't eat yer,
And so we mocked your humble destiny –
Yet life was merry, was it not, oh rat?
It must have been to one so sleek and fat.

JOHN PEALE BISHOP
1892–1944

In the Dordogne

We stood up before day
and shaved by metal mirrors
in the faint flame of a faulty candle.

And we hurried down the wide stone stairs
with a clirr of spurr chains
on stone. And we thought
when the cocks crew
that the ghosts of a dead dawn
would rise and be off. But they stayed
under the window, crouched on the staircase,
the window now the colour of morning.

The colonel slept in the bed of Sully,
slept on: but we descended
and saw in a niche in the white wall
a Virgin and child, serene
who were stone: we saw sycamore:
three aged mages
scattering gifts of gold.
But when the wind blew, there were autumn
    odours
and the shadowed trees
had the dapplings of young fawns.

And each day one died or another
died: each week we sent out thousands
that returned by hundreds
wounded or gassed. And those that died
we buried close to the old wall
within a stone's throw of Perigord
under the tower of the troubadours.

And because we had courage;
because there was courage and youth
ready to be wasted; because we endured
and were prepared for all the endurance;
we thought something must come of it:
that the Virgin would raise her child and smile;
the trees gather up their gold and go;
that courage would avail something
and something we had never lost
be regained through wastage, by dying,
by burying the others under the English tower.

The colonel slept on in the bed of Sully
under the ravelling curtains: the leaves fell
and were blown away: the young men rotted
under the shadow of the tower
in a land of small clear silent streams
where the coming on of evening is
the letting down of blue and azure veils
over the clear and silent streams
delicately bordered by poplars.

EDMUND BLUNDEN
1896–1974

The Zonnebeke Road

Morning, if this late withered light can claim
Some kindred with that merry flame
Which the young day was wont to fling through
    space!
Agony stares from each grey face.
And yet the day is come; stand down! stand down!
Your hands unclasp from rifles while you can;
The frost has pierced them to the bended bone?
Why, see old Stevens there, that iron man,
Melting the ice to shave his grotesque chin!
Go ask him, shall we win?
I never liked this bay, some foolish fear
Caught me the first time that I came in here;
That dugout fallen in awakes, perhaps,
Some formless haunting of some corpse's chaps.
True, and wherever we have held the line,
There were such corners, seeming-saturnine
For no good cause.
                Now where Haymarket starts,
That is no place for soldiers with weak hearts;
The minenwerfers have it to the inch.
Look, how the snow-dust whisks along the road
Piteous and silly; the stones themselves must flinch
In this east wind; the low sky like a load
Hangs over, a dead-weight. But what a pain
Must gnaw where its clay cheek
Crushes the shell-chopped trees that fang the plain –
The ice-bound throat gulps out a gargoyle shriek.
That wretched wire before the village line
Rattles like rusty brambles or dead bine,
And there the daylight oozes into dun;

Black pillars, those are trees where roadways run.
Even Ypres now would warm our souls; fond fool,
Our tour's but one night old, seven more to cool!
O screaming dumbness, O dull clashing death,
Shreds of dead grass and willows, homes and men,
Watch as you will, men clench their chattering teeth
And freeze you back with that one hope, disdain.

1916 Seen from 1921

Tired with dull grief, grown old before my day,
I sit in solitude and only hear
Long silent laughters, murmurings of dismay,
The lost intensities of hope and fear;
In those old marshes yet the rifles lie,
On the thin breastwork flutter the grey rags,
The very books I read are there – and I
Dead as the men I loved, wait while life drags

Its wounded length from those sad streets of war
Into green places here, that were my own;
But now what once was mine is mine no more,
I seek such neighbours here and I find none.
With such strong gentleness and tireless will
Those ruined houses seared themselves in me,
Passionate I look for their dumb story still,
And the charred stub outspeaks the living tree.

I rise up at the singing of a bird
And scarcely knowing slink along the lane,
I dare not give a soul a look or word
Where all have homes and none's at home in vain:
Deep red the rose burned in the grim redoubt,
The self-sown wheat around was like a flood,
In the hot path the lizard lolled time out,
The saints in broken shrines were bright as blood.

Sweet Mary's shrine between the sycamores!
There we would go, my friend of friends and I,
And snatch long moments from the grudging wars,
Whose dark made light intense to see them by.
Shrewd bit the morning fog, the whining shots
Spun from the wrangling wire; then in warm swoon
The sun hushed all but the cool orchard plots,
We crept in the tall grass and slept till noon.

Two Voices

'There's something in the air,' he said
    In the farm parlour cool and bare;
Plain words, which in his hearers bred
    A tumult, yet in silence there
All waited; wryly gay, he left the phrase,
Ordered the march, and bade us go our ways.

'We're going South, man'; as he spoke
    The howitzer with huge ping-bang
Racked the light hut; as thus he broke
    The death-news, bright the skylarks sang;
He took his riding-crop and humming went
Among the apple-trees all bloom and scent.

Now far withdraws the roaring night
    Which wrecked our flower after the first
Of those two voices; misty light
    Shrouds Thiepval Wood and all its worst;
But still 'There's something in the air' I hear,
And still 'We're going South, man,' deadly near.

ROBERT BRIDGES
1844–1930

The Chivalry of the Sea

Dedicated to the memory of Charles Fisher
late student of Christ Church, Oxford

Over the warring waters, beneath the wandering skies,
The heart of Britain roameth, the Chivalry of the sea,
Where Spring never bringeth a flower, nor bird singeth in a
    tree;
Far, afar, O beloved, beyond the sight of our eyes,
Over the warring waters, beneath the stormy skies.

Staunch and valiant-hearted, to whom our toil were play,
Ye man with armour'd patience, the bulwarks night and day,
Or on your iron coursers plough shuddering through the
    Bay,
Or 'neath the deluge drive the skirmishing sharks of war:
Venturous boys who leapt on the pinnace and row'd from
    shore,
A mother's tear in the eye, a swift farewell to say,
And a great glory at heart that none can take away.

Seldom is your home-coming; for aye your pennon flies
In unrecorded exploits on the tumultuous wave;
Till, in the storm of battle, fast-thundering upon the foe,
Ye add your kindred names to the heroes of long ago,
And 'mid the blasting wrack, in the glad sudden death of the
    brave,
Ye are gone to return no more. – Idly our tears arise;
Too proud for praise as ye lie in your unvisited grave,
The wide-warring water, under the starry skies.

Lord Kitchener

Unflinching hero, watchful to forsee
   And face thy country's peril wheresoe'er,
   Directing war and peace with equal care,
Till by long duty ennobled thou wert he
Whom England call'd and bade: 'Set my arm free
   To obey my will and save my honour fair,' –
   What day the foe presumed on her despair
And she herself had trust in none but thee:

Among Herculean deeds the miracle
   That mass'd the labour of ten years in one
   Shall be thy monument. Thy work was done
Ere we could thank thee; and the high sea swell
Surgeth unheeding where thy proud ship fell
By the lone Orkneys, at the set of sun.

Trafalgar Square

Fool that I was! my heart was sore,
Yea, sick for the myriad wounded men,
The maim'd in the war: I had grief for each one:
And I came in the gay September sun
To the open smile of Trafalgar Square,
Where many a lad with a limb foredone
Loll'd by the lion-guarded column
That holdeth Nelson statued thereon
Upright in the air.

The Parliament towers, and the Abbey towers,
The white Horseguards and grey Whitehall,
He looketh on all,
Past Somerset House and the river's bend
To the pillar'd dome of St Paul,
That slumbers, confessing God's solemn blessing
On Britain's glory, to keep it ours –
While children true her prowess renew
And throng from the ends of the earth to defend
Freedom and honour – till Earth shall end.

The gentle unjealous Shakespeare, I trow,
In his country grave of peaceful fame
Must feel exiled from life and glow,
If he thinks of this man with his warrior claim,
Who looketh on London as if 'twere his own,
As he standeth in stone, aloft and alone,
Sailing the sky, with one arm and one eye.

RUPERT BROOKE

1887–1915. Died, Greece, 21st April

1914: I *Peace*

Now, God be thanked Who has matched us with His hour,
  And caught our youth, and wakened us from sleeping,
With hand made sure, clear eye, and sharpened power,
  To turn, as swimmers into cleanness leaping,
Glad from a world grown old and cold and weary,
  Leave the sick hearts that honour could not move,
And half-men, and their dirty songs and dreary,
  And all the little emptiness of love!

Oh! we, who have known shame, we have found release
    there,
  Where there's no ill, no grief, but sleep has mending,
    Naught broken save this body, lost but breath;
Nothing to shake the laughing heart's long peace there
  But only agony, and that has ending;
    And the worst friend and enemy is but Death.

II *Safety*

Dear! of all happy in the hour, most blest
  He who has found our hid security,
Assured in the dark tides of the world at rest,
  And heard our word, 'Who is so safe as we?'
We have found safety with all things undying,
  The winds, and morning, tears of men and mirth,
The deep night, and birds singing, and clouds flying,
  And sleep, and freedom, and the autumnal earth.
We have built a house that is not for Time's throwing.
  We have gained a peace unshaken by pain for ever.
War knows no power. Safe shall be my going,
  Secretly armed against all death's endeavour;
Safe though all safety's lost; safe where men fall;
And if these poor limbs die, safest of all.

III *The Dead*

Blow out, you bugles, over the rich Dead!
   There's none of these so lonely and poor of old,
   But, dying, has made us rarer gifts than gold.
These laid the world away; poured out the red
Sweet wine of youth; gave up the years to be
   Of work and joy, and that unhoped serene,
   That men call age; and those who would have been,
Their sons, they gave, their immortality.

Blow, bugles, blow! They brought us, for our dearth,
   Holiness, lacked so long, and Love, and Pain.
Honour has come back, as a king, to earth,
   And paid his subjects with a royal wage;
And Nobleness walks in our ways again;
   And we have come into our heritage.

IV *The Dead*

These hearts were woven of human joys and cares,
   Washed marvellously with sorrow, swift to mirth.
The years had given them kindness. Dawn was theirs,
   And sunset, and the colours of the earth.
These had seen movement, and heard music; known
   Slumber and waking; loved; gone proudly friended;
Felt the quick stir of wonder; sat alone;
   Touched flowers and furs and cheeks. All this is
     ended.

There are waters blown by changing winds to laughter
And lit by the rich skies, all day. And after,
   Frost, with a gesture, stays the waves that dance
And wandering loveliness. He leaves a white
   Unbroken glory, a gathered radiance,
A width, a shining peace, under the night.

v *The Soldier*

If I should die, think only this of me:
    That there's some corner of a foreign field
That is for ever England. There shall be
    In that rich earth a richer dust concealed;
A dust whom England bore, shaped, made aware,
    Gave, once, her flowers to love, her ways to roam,
A body of England's, breathing English air,
    Washed by the rivers, blest by suns of home.

And think, this heart, all evil shed away,
    A pulse in the eternal mind, no less
        Gives somewhere back the thoughts by England
            given;
Her sights and sounds; dreams happy as her day;
    And laughter, learnt of friends; and gentleness,
        In hearts at peace, under an English heaven.

G. K. CHESTERTON
1874–1936

Elegy in a Country Churchyard

The men that worked for England
They have their graves at home:
And bees and birds of England
About the cross can roam.

But they that fought for England,
Following a falling star,
Alas, alas for England
They have their graves afar.

And they that rule in England,
In stately conclave met,
Alas, alas for England
They have no graves as yet.

LESLIE COULSON

1889–1916
Died of wounds, the Somme, 8th October

War

Where war has left its wake of whitened bone,
Soft stems of summer grass shall wave again,
And all the blood that war has ever strewn
        Is but a passing stain.

Who Made the Law?

Who made the Law that men should die in meadows?
Who spake the word that blood should splash in lanes?
Who gave it forth that gardens should be bone-yards?
Who spread the hills with flesh, and blood, and brains?
Who made the Law?

Who made the Law that Death should stalk the village?
Who spake the word to kill among the sheaves?
Who gave it forth that death should lurk in hedgerows?
Who flung the dead among the fallen leaves?
Who made the Law?

Those who return shall find that peace endures,
Find old things old, and know the things they knew,
Walk in the garden, slumber by the fireside,
Share the peace of dawn, and dream amid the dew –
Those who return.

Those who return shall till the ancient pastures,
Clean-hearted men shall guide the plough-horse reins,
Some shall grow apples and flowers in the valleys,
Some shall go courting in summer down the lanes –
THOSE WHO RETURN.

But who made the Law? the Trees shall whisper to him:
'See, see the blood – the splashes on our bark!'
Walking the meadows, he shall hear bones crackle,
And fleshless mouths shall gibber in silent lanes at dark.
Who made the Law?

Who made the Law? At noon upon the hillside
His ears shall hear a moan, his cheeks shall feel a breath,
And all along the valleys, past gardens, croft, and
     homesteads,
HE who made the Law,
     He who made the Law,
He who made the Law shall walk along with Death.
     WHO made the Law?

FORD MADOX FORD

1873–1939

That Exploit of Yours

I meet two soldiers sometimes here in Hell
The one, with a tear in the seat of his red pantaloons
Was stuck by a pitchfork,
Climbing a wall to steal apples.

The second has a seeming silver helmet,
Having died from the fall of his horse on some tram-lines
In Dortmund.

These two
Meeting in the vaulted and vaporous caverns of Hell
Exclaim always in identical tones:
'I at least have done my duty to Society and the
    Fatherland!'
It is strange how the cliché prevails . . .
For I will bet my hat that you who sent me here to Hell
Are saying the selfsame words at this very moment
Concerning that exploit of yours.

GILBERT FRANKAU
1884–1952

The Deserter

'I'm sorry I done it, Major.'
We bandaged the livid face;
And led him out, ere the wan sun rose,
To die his death of disgrace.

The bolt-heads locked to the cartridge;
The rifles steadied to rest,
As cold stock nestled at colder cheek
And foresight lined on the breast.

'*Fire!*' called the Sergeant-Major.
The muzzles flamed as he spoke:
And the shameless soul of a nameless man
Went up in the cordite-smoke.

JOHN FREEMAN
1880–1929

Armistice Day

Birds stayed not their singing,
The heart its beating,
The blood its steady coursing
  The child in the dark womb
Stirred; dust settled in the tomb.

Old wounds were still smarting,
Echoes were hollow-sounding,
New desires still upspringing.
  No silent Armistice might stay
Life and Death wrangling in the old way.

Earth's pulse still was beating,
The bright stars circling;
Only our tongues were hushing.
  While Time ticked silent on, men drew
A deeper breath than passion knew.

JOHN GALSWORTHY
1867–1933

The Soldier Speaks

If courage thrives on reeking slaughter,
   And he who kills is lord
Of beauty and of loving laughter –
   Gird on me a sword!
If death be dearest comrade proven,
   If life be coward's mate,
If Nazareth of dreams be woven –
   Give me fighter's fate!

     *   *   *

If God be thrilled by a battle cry,
   If He can bless the moaning fight,
If when the trampling charge goes by
   God himself is the leading Knight;
If God laughs when the gun thunders,
   If He yells when the bullet sings –
Then my stoic soul but wonders
   How great God can do such things!

     *   *   *

The white gulls wheeling over the plough,
   The sun, the reddening trees –
We being enemies, I and thou,
   There is no meaning to these.
There is no flight on the wings of Spring,
   No scent in the summer rose;
The roundelays that the blackbirds sing –
   There is no meaning in those!

If you must kill me – why the lark,
   The hawthorn bud, and the corn?
Why do the stars bedew the dark?
   Why is the blossom born?
If I must kill you – why the kiss
   Which made you? There is no why !
If it be true we were born for this –
   Pitiful Love, Good-bye!

*   *   *

Not for the God of battles!
For Honour, Freedom and Right.
And saving of Gentle Beauty,
We have gone down to fight!

Valley of the Shadow

God, I am travelling out to death's sea,
   I, who exulted in sunshine and laughter,
Thought not of dying – death is such waste of me!
   Grant me one comfort: Leave not the hereafter
Of mankind to war, as though I had died not –
   I, who in battle, my comrade's arm linking,
Shouted and sang – life in my pulses hot
   Throbbing and dancing! Let not my sinking
In dark be for naught, my death a vain thing!
   God, let me know it the end of man's fever!
Make my last breath a bugle call, carrying
   Peace o'er the valleys and cold hills, for ever!

JULIAN GRENFELL

1888–1915
Died of wounds, Boulogne, 26th May

Prayer for Those on the Staff

Fighting in mud we turn to Thee,
In these dread times of battle, Lord,
To keep us safe, if so may be,
From shrapnel, snipers, shell, and sword.

But not on us, for we are men
Of meaner clay, who fight in clay,
But on the Staff, the Upper Ten,
Depends the issue of the Day.

The Staff is working with its brains,
While we are sitting in the trench;
The Staff the universe ordains
(Subject to Thee and General French.)

God help the Staff – especially
The young ones, many of them sprung
From our high aristocracy;
Their task is hard, and they are young.

O Lord, who mad'st all things to be,
And madest some things very good,
Please keep the extra A.D.C.
From horrid scenes, and sight of blood.

See that his eggs are newly laid,
Not tinged as some of them – with green;
And let no nasty draughts invade
The windows of his limousine.

When he forgets to buy the bread,
When there are no more minerals,
Preserve his smooth well-oiled head
From wrath of caustic Generals.

O Lord, who mad'st all things to be,
And hatest nothing thou have made,
Please keep the extra A.D.C.
Out of the sun and in the shade.

Into Battle

The naked earth is warm with spring,
    And with green grass and bursting trees
Leans to the sun's gaze glorying,
    And quivers in the sunny breeze;
And life is colour and warmth and light,
    And a striving evermore for these;
And he is dead who will not fight;
    And who dies fighting has increase.

The fighting man shall from the sun
    Take warmth, and life from the glowing earth;
Speed with the light-foot winds to run,
    And with the trees to newer birth;
And find, when fighting shall be done,
    Great rest, and fullness after dearth.

All the bright company of Heaven
    Hold him in their high comradeship,
The Dog-Star, and the Sisters Seven,
    Orion's Belt and sworded hip.

The woodland trees that stand together,
    They stand to him each one a friend;
They gently speak in the windy weather;
    They guide to valley and ridge's end.

The kestrel hovering by day,
    And the little owls that call by night,
Bid him be swift and keen as they,
    As keen of ear, as swift of sight.

The blackbird sings to him, 'Brother, brother,
    If this be the last song you shall sing,
Sing well, for you may not sing another;
    Brother, sing.'

In dreary, doubtful, waiting hours,
    Before the brazen frenzy starts,
The horses show him nobler powers;
    O patient eyes, courageous hearts!

And when the burning moment breaks,
    And all things else are out of mind,
And only joy of battle takes
    Him by the throat, and makes him blind,

Through joy and blindness he shall know,
    Not caring much to know, that still
Nor lead nor steel shall reach him, so
    That it be not the Destined Will.

The thundering line of battle stands,
    And in the air death moans and sings;
But Day shall clasp him with strong hands,
    And Night shall fold him in soft wings.

IVOR GURNEY
1890–1937

Ballad of the Three Spectres

As I went up by Ovillers
   In mud and water cold to the knee,
There went three jeering fleering spectres,
   That walked abreast and talked of me.

The first said, 'Here's a right brave soldier
   That walks the dark unfearingly;
Soon he'll come back on a fine stretcher,
   And laughing for a nice Blighty.'

The second, 'Read his face, old comrade,
   No kind of lucky chance I see;
One day he'll freeze in mud to the marrow,
   Then look his last on Picardy.'

Though bitter the word of these first twain
   Curses the third spat venomously;
'He'll stay untouched till the war's last dawning
   Then live one hour of agony.'

Liars the first two were. Behold me
   At sloping arms by one-two-three;
Waiting the time I shall discover
   Whether the third spake verity.

To His Love

He's gone, and all our plans
  Are useless indeed.
We'll walk no more on Cotswold
  Where the sheep feed
  Quietly and take no heed.

His body that was so quick
  Is not as you
Knew it, on Severn river
  Under the blue
  Driving our small boat through.

You would not know him now . . .
  But still he died
Nobly, so cover him over
  With violets of pride
  Purple from Severn side.

Cover him, cover him soon!
  And with thick-set
Masses of memoried flowers –
  Hide that red wet
  Thing I must somehow forget.

The Silent One

Who died on the wires, and hung there, one of two –
Who for his hours of life had chattered through
Infinite lovely chatter of Bucks accent:
Yet faced unbroken wires; stepped over, and went
A noble fool, faithful to his stripes – and ended.
But I weak, hungry, and willing only for the chance
Of line – to fight in the line, lay down under unbroken
Wires, and saw the flashes and kept unshaken,
Till the politest voice – a finicking accent, said:
'Do you think you might crawl through, there: there's a
      hole.'
Darkness, shot at: I smiled, as politely replied –
'I'm afraid not, Sir.' There was no hole no way to be seen
Nothing but chance of death, after tearing of clothes
Kept flat, and watched the darkness, hearing bullets
      whizzing –
And thought of music – and swore deep heart's deep
      oaths
(Polite to God) and retreated and came on again,
Again retreated – and a second time faced the screen.

The Bohemians

Certain people would not clean their buttons,
Nor polish buckles after latest fashions,
Preferred their hair long, putties comfortable,
Barely escaping hanging, indeed hardly able,
In Bridge and smoking without army cautions
Spending hours that sped like evil for quickness,
(While others burnished brasses, earned promotions)
These were those ones who jested in the trench,
While others argued of army ways, and wrenched
What little soul they had still further from shape,
And died off one by one, or became officers
Without the first of dream, the ghost of notions
Of ever becoming soldiers, or smart and neat,
Surprised as ever to find the army capable
Of sounding 'Lights out' to break a game of Bridge,
As to fear candles would set a barn alight.
In Artois or Picardy they lie – free of useless fashions.

War Books

What did they expect of our toil and extreme
Hunger – the perfect drawing of a heart's dream?
Did they look for a book of wrought art's perfection,
Who promised no reading, nor praise, nor publication?
Out of the heart's sickness the spirit wrote
For delight, or to escape hunger, or of war's worst anger,
When the guns died to silence and men would gather sense
Somehow together, and find this was life indeed,
And praise another's nobleness, or to Cotswold get hence.
There we wrote – Corbie Ridge – or in Gonnehem at rest.
Or Fauquissart or world's death songs, ever the best.
One made sorrows' praise passing the Church where silence
Opened for the long quivering strokes of the bell –
Another wrote all soldiers' praise, and of France and night's
    stars.
Served his guns, got immortality, and died well.
But Ypres played another trick with its danger on me,
Kept still the needing and loving of action body;
Gave no candles, and nearly killed me twice as well,
And no souvenirs though I risked my life in the stuck tanks,
Yet there was praise of Ypres, love came sweet in hospital
And old Flanders went under to long ages of plays thought in
    my pages.

Strange Hells

There are strange Hells within the minds War made
Not so often, not so humiliatingly afraid
As one would have expected – the racket and fear guns
    made.

One Hell the Gloucester soldiers they quite put out;
Their first bombardment, when in combined black shout
Of fury, guns aligned, they ducked low their heads
And sang with diaphragms fixed beyond all dreads,
That tin and stretched-wire tinkle, that blither of tune;
'Après la guerre fini' till Hell all had come down,
Twelve-inch, six-inch, and eighteen pounders hammering
    Hell's thunders.

Where are they now on State-doles, or showing shop patterns
Or walking town to town sore in borrowed tatterns
Or begged. Some civic routine one never learns.
The heart burns – but has to keep out of face how heart
    burns.

THOMAS HARDY
1840–1928

Men Who March Away

Song of the Soldiers

What of the faith and fire within us
    Men who march away
    Ere the barn-cocks say
    Night is growing grey,
Leaving all that here can win us;
What of the faith and fire within us
    Men who march away?

Is it a purblind prank, O think you,
    Friend with the musing eye,
    Who watch us stepping by
    With doubt and dolorous sigh?
Can much pondering so hoodwink you!
Is it a purblind prank, O think you,
    Friend with the musing eye?

Nay. We well see what we are doing,
    Though some may not see –
    Dalliers as they be –
    England's need are we;
Her distress would leave us rueing:
Nay. We well see what we are doing,
    Though some may not see!

In our heart of hearts believing
    Victory crowns the just,
    And that braggarts must
    Surely bite the dust,
Press we to the field ungrieving,
In our heart of hearts believing
    Victory crowns the just.

Hence the faith and fire within us
    Men who march away
    Ere the barn-cocks say
    Night is growing grey,
Leaving all that here can win us;
Hence the faith and fire within us
    Men who march away.

Channel Firing

That night your great guns, unawares,
Shook all our coffins as we lay,
And broke the chancel window-squares,
We thought it was the Judgment-day

And sat upright. While drearisome
Arose the howl of wakened hounds:
The mouse let fall the altar-crumb,
The worms drew back into the mounds,

The glebe cow drooled. Till God called, 'No;
It's gunnery practice out at sea
Just as before you went below;
The world is as it used to be:

'All nations striving strong to make
Red war yet redder. Mad as hatters
They do no more for Christés sake
Than you who are helpless in such matters.

'That this is not the judgement-hour
For some of them's a blessed thing,
For if it were they'd have to scour
Hell's floor for so much threatening . . .

'Ha, ha. It will be warmer when
I blow the trumpet (if indeed
I ever do; for you are men,
And rest eternal sorely need).'

So down we lay again. 'I wonder,
Will the world ever saner be,'
Said one, 'than when He sent us under
In our indifferent century!'

And many a skeleton shook his head.
'Instead of preaching forty year,'
My neighbour Parson Thirdly said,
'I wish I had stuck to pipes and beer.'

Again the guns disturbed the hour,
Roaring their readiness to avenge,
As far inland as Stourton Tower,
And Camelot, and starlit Stonehenge.

W. N. HODGSON

1893–1916
Killed, the Somme, 1st July

Before Action

By all the glories of the day
  And the cool evening's benison,
By that last sunset touch that lay
  Upon the hills when day was done,
By beauty lavishly outpoured
  And blessings carelessly received,
By all the days that I have lived
  Make me a soldier, Lord.

By all of all man's hopes and fears,
  And all the wonders poets sing,
The laughter of unclouded years,
  And every sad and lovely thing;
By the romantic ages stored
  With high endeavour that was his,
By all his mad catastrophes
  Make me a man, O Lord.

I, that on my familiar hill
  Saw with uncomprehending eyes
A hundred of Thy sunsets spill
  Their fresh and sanguine sacrifice,
Ere the sun swings his noonday sword
  Must say good-bye to all of this; –
By all delights that I shall miss,
  Help me to die, O Lord.

A. E. HOUSMAN
1859–1936

Here Dead Lie We

Here dead lie we because we did not choose
To live and shame the land from which we sprung.
Life, to be sure, is nothing much to lose;
But young men think it is, and we were young.

Epitaph on an Army of Mercenaries

These, in the day when heaven was falling,
   The hour when earth's foundations fled,
Followed their mercenary calling
   And took their wages and are dead.

Their shoulders held the sky suspended;
   They stood, and earth's foundations stay;
What God abandoned, these defended,
   And saved the sum of things for pay.

T. E. HULME

1883–1917
Killed, Belgium, 28th September

Trenches: St Eloi

Over the flat slope of St Eloi
A wide wall of sandbags.
Night,
In the silence desultory men
Pottering over small fires, cleaning
    their mess-tins:
To and fro, from the lines,
Men walk as on Piccadilly,
Making paths in the dark,
Through scattered dead horses,
Over a dead Belgian's belly.

PHILIP JOHNSTONE

'High Wood' was first published in *The Nation*,
16th February 1918

High Wood

Ladies and gentlemen, this is High Wood,
Called by the French, Bois des Fourneaux,
The famous spot which in Nineteen-Sixteen,
July, August and September was the scene
Of long and bitterly contested strife,
By reason of its High commanding site.
Observe the effect of shell-fire in the trees
Standing and fallen; here is wire; this trench
For months inhabited, twelve times changed hands;
(They soon fall in), used later as a grave.
It has been said on good authority
That in the fighting for this patch of wood
Were killed somewhere above eight thousand men,
Of whom the greater part were buried here,
This mound on which you stand being . . .

                                 Madame, please,
You are requested kindly not to touch
Or take away the Company's property
As souvenirs; you'll find we have on sale
A large variety, all guaranteed.
As I was saying, all is as it was,
This is an unknown British officer,
The tunic having lately rotted off.
Please follow me – this way . . .

                             the *path*, sir, *please*,
The ground which was secured at great expense
The Company keeps absolutely untouched,
And in that dug-out (genuine) we provide
Refreshments at a reasonable rate.
You are requested not to leave about
Paper, or ginger-beer bottles, or orange-peel,
There are waste-paper baskets at the gate.

RUDYARD KIPLING
1865–1936

For all we have and are

For all we have and are,
For all our children's fate,
Stand up and meet the war.
The Hun is at the gate!
Our world has passed away
In wantonness o'erthrown.
There is nothing left today
But steel and fire and stone.

    Though all we knew depart,
    The old commandments stand:
    'In courage keep your heart,
    In strength lift up your hand.'

Once more we hear the word
That sickened earth of old:
'No law except the sword
Unsheathed and uncontrolled,'

Once more it knits mankind,
Once more the nations go
To meet and break and bind
A crazed and driven foe.

Comfort, content, delight –
The ages' slow-bought gain –
They shrivelled in a night,
Only ourselves remain
To face the naked days
In silent fortitude,
Through perils and dismays
Renewed and re-renewed.

Though all we made depart,
 The old commandments stand:
'In patience keep your heart,
 In strength lift up your hand.'

No easy hopes or lies
 Shall bring us to our goal,
But iron sacrifice
 of body, will, and soul.
There is but one task for all –
 For each one life to give.
Who stands if Freedom fall?
Who dies if England live?

The Choice

1917. The American Spirit Speaks

To the judge of Right and Wrong
 With Whom fulfilment lies
Our purpose and our power belong,
 Our faith and sacrifice.

Let Freedom's Land rejoice!
 Our ancient bonds are riven;
Once more to us the eternal choice
 Of Good or Ill is given.

Not at a little cost,
 Hardly by prayers or tears,
Shall we recover the road we lost
 In the drugged and doubting years.

But after the fires and the wrath,
 But, after searching and pain,
His Mercy opens us a path
 To live with ourselves again.

In the Gates of Death rejoice!
    We see and hold the good –
Bear witness, Earth, we have made our choice
    With Freedom's brotherhood!

Then praise the Lord Most High
    Whose Strength hath saved us whole,
Who bade us choose that the Flesh should die
    And not the living Soul!

To the God in man displayed –
    Where e'er we see that Birth,
Be love and understanding paid
    As never yet on earth!

To the Spirit that moves in Man,
    On Whom all worlds depend,
Be Glory since our world began
    And service to the end!

Gethsemane (1914–18)

The Garden called Gethsemane
    In Picardy it was,
And there the people came to see
    The English soldiers pass.

We used to pass – we used to pass
    Or halt, as it might be,
And ship our masks in case of gas
    Beyond Gethsemane.

The Garden called Gethsemane,
    It held a pretty lass,
But all the time she talked to me
    I prayed my cup might pass.

The officer sat on the chair,
    The men lay on the grass,
And all the time we halted there
    I prayed my cup might pass.

It didn't pass – it didn't pass –
    It didn't pass from me.
I drank it when we met the gas
    Beyond Gethsemane!

Common Form

If any question why we died,
Tell them, because our fathers lied.

A Dead Statesman

I could not dig; I dared not rob:
Therefore I lied to please the mob.
Now all my lies are proved untrue
And I must face the men I slew.
What tale shall serve me here among
Mine angry and defrauded young?

W. S. S. LYON
1893–1915
Killed, Ypres, 8th May

I tracked a dead man down a trench

I tracked a dead man down a trench,
　I knew not he was dead.
They told me he had gone that way,
　And there his foot-marks led.

The trench was long and close and curved,
　It seemed without an end;
And as I threaded each new bay
　I thought to see my friend.

I went there stooping to the ground.
　For, should I raise my head,
Death watched to spring; and how should then
　A dead man find the dead?

At last I saw his back. He crouched
　As still as still could be,
And when I called his name aloud
　He did not answer me.

The floor-way of the trench was wet
　Where he was crouching dead;
The water of the pool was brown,
　And round him it was red.

I stole up softly where he stayed
　With head hung down all slack,
And on his shoulders laid my hands
　And drew him gently back.

And then, as I had guessed, I saw
　His head, and how the crown –
I saw then why he crouched so still,
　And why his head hung down.

JOHN McCRAE
1872–1918

In Flanders Fields

In Flanders fields the poppies blow
Between the crosses, row on row
   That mark our place; and in the sky
   The larks, still bravely singing, fly
Scarce heard amid the guns below.

We are the Dead. Short days ago
We lived, felt dawn, saw sunset glow,
   Loved and were loved, and now we lie
      In Flanders fields.

Take up our quarrel with the foe:
To you from failing hands we throw
   The torch; be yours to hold it high.
   If ye break faith with us who die
We shall not sleep, though poppies grow
      In Flanders fields.

E. A. MACKINTOSH

1893–1917
Killed, Cambrai, 21st November

Sniper Sandy

To the Tune: Sister Susie's sewing shirts for soldiers.

Sandy Mac the sniper is a-sniping from his loop-hole,
With a telescopic rifle he is looking for a Hun.
If he sees a sniper lurking, or a working-party working,
At once he opens fire on them, and bags them every one.
And when you come into our trench, by night-time or by
    day.
We take you to his loop-hole, and we point to him and
    say –

   Chorus –
'Sniper Sandy's slaying Saxon soldiers,
And Saxon soldiers seldom show but Sandy slays a few,
And every day the Bosches put up little wooden crosses
In the cemetery for Saxon soldiers Sniper Sandy slew.'

Now in the German trenches there's a sniper they call
    Hermann,
A stout and stolid Saxon with a healthy growth of beard,
And Hermann with his rifle is the pride of every German,
Until our Sandy gets on him, and Hermann gets afeared,
For when he hears the bullets come he slides down to the
    ground,
And trembling he gasps out to his comrades all around –

   Chorus –
'Sniper Sandy's slaying Saxon soldiers,
And Saxon soldiers seldom show but Sandy slays a few,
And every day the Bosches put up little wooden crosses
In the cemetery for Saxon soldiers Sniper Sandy slew.'

The Seaforths got so proud of Sandy's prowess with his
     rifle,
They drew up a report on him and sent it to the Corps,
And ninety-seven was his bag – it doesn't seem a trifle –
But Sandy isn't certain that it wasn't rather more,
And when Sir John French heard of it, he broke into a
     laugh,
And rubbed his hands and chuckled to the Chief of
     General Staff –

  Chorus –
'Sniper Sandy's slaying Saxon soldiers,
And Saxon soldiers seldom show but Sandy slays a few,
And every day the Bosches put up little wooden crosses
In the cemetery for Saxon soldiers Sniper Sandy slew.'

A. J. MANN
1896–1917
Died of wounds, Arras, 10th April

The Soldier

'Tis strange to look on a man that is dead
As he lies in the shell-swept hell,
And to think that the poor black battered corpse
Once lived like you and was well.

'Tis stranger far when you come to think
That you may be soon like him . . .
And it's Fear that tugs at your trembling soul,
A Fear that is weird and grim!

FREDERIC MANNING
1882–1935

The Face

Guillemont

Out of the smoke of men's wrath,
The red mist of anger,
Suddenly,
As a wraith of sleep,
A boy's face, white and tense,
Convulsed with terror and hate,
The lips trembling . . .

Then a red smear, falling . . .
I thrust aside the cloud, as it were tangible,
Blinded with a mist of blood.
The face cometh again
As a wraith of sleep:
A boy's face, delicate and blond,
The very mask of God,
Broken.

Grotesque

These are the damned circles Dante trod,
Terrible in hopelessness,
But even skulls have their humour,
An eyeless and sardonic mockery:
And we,
Sitting with streaming eyes in the acrid smoke,
That murks our foul, damp billet,
Chant bitterly, with raucous voices
As a choir of frogs
In hideous irony, our patriotic songs.

The Sign

We are here in a wood of little beeches:
And the leaves are like black lace
Against a sky of nacre.

One bough of clear promise
Across the moon.

It is in this wise that God speaketh unto me.
He layeth hands of healing upon my flesh,
Stilling it in an eternal peace,
Until my soul reaches out myriad and infinite
    hands
Toward Him,
And is eased of its hunger.

And I know that this passes:
This implacable fury and torment of men,
As a thing insensate and vain:
And the stillness hath said unto me,
Over the tumult of sounds and shaken flame,
Out of the terrible beauty of wrath,
I alone am eternal.

One bough of clear promise
Across the moon.

The Trenches

Endless lanes sunken in the clay,
Bays, and traverses, fringed with wasted herbage,
Seed-pods of blue scabious, and some lingering blooms;
And the sky, seen as from a well,
Brilliant with frosty stars.
We stumble, cursing, on the slippery duck-boards.
Goaded like the damned by some invisible wrath,
A will stronger than weariness, stronger than animal fear,
Implacable and monotonous.

Here a shaft, slanting, and below
A dusty and flickering light from one feeble candle
And prone figures sleeping uneasily,
Murmuring,
And men who cannot sleep,
With faces impassive as masks,
Bright, feverish eyes, and drawn lips,
Sad, pitiless, terrible faces,
Each an incarnate curse.

Here in a bay, a helmeted sentry
Silent and motionless, watching while two sleep,
And he sees before him
With indifferent eyes the blasted and torn land
Peopled with stiff prone forms, stupidly rigid,
As tho' they had not been men.

Dead are the lips where love laughed or sang,
The hands of youth eager to lay hold of life,
Eyes that have laughed to eyes,
And these were begotten,
O Love, and lived lightly, and burnt
With the lust of a man's first strength: ere they were rent,
Almost at unawares, savagely; and strewn
In bloody fragments, to be the carrion
Of rats and crows.

And the sentry moves not, searching
Night for menace with weary eyes.

NEIL MUNRO

1864–1930

Pipes in Arras

In the burgh toun of Arras,
    When gloaming had come on,
Fifty pipers played Retreat
    As if they had been one,
And the Grande Place of Arras
    Hummed with the Highland drone!

Then to the ravaged burgh,
    Champed into dust and Sand,
Came with the pipers' playing,
    Out or their own beloved land,
Sea-sounds that moan for sorrow
    On a dispeopled strand.

There are in France no voices
    To speak of simple things,
And tell how winds will whistle
    Through palaces of kings;
Now came the truth to Arras
    In the chanter's warblings:

'O build in pride your towers,
    But think not they will last;
The tall tower and the shealing
    Alike must meet the blast,
And the world is strewn with shingle
    From dwellings of the past.'

But to the Grande Place, Arras,
    Came, too, the hum of bees,
That suck the sea-pink's sweetness
    From isles of the Hebrides,
And in Iona fashion
    Homes mid old effigies:

'Our cells the monks demolished
    To make their mead of yore,
And still though we be ravished
    Each Autumn of our store,
While the sun lasts, and the flower,
    Tireless we'll gather more.'

Up then and spake with twitt'rings
    Out of the chanter reed,
Birds that each Spring to Appin,
    Over the oceans speed,
And in its ruined castles
    Make love again and breed:

'Already see our brothers
    Build in the tottering fane!
Though France should be a desert,
    While love and Spring remain,
Men will come back to Arras,
    And build and weave again.'

So played the pipes in Arras
    Their Gaelic symphony,
Sweet with old wisdom gathered
    In isles of the Highland sea,
And eastward towards Cambrai
    Roared the artillery.

Lochaber No More

Farewell to Lochaber, farewell to the glen,
  No more will he wander Lochaber again.
Lochaber no more! Lochaber no more!
  The lad will return to Lochaber no more!
The trout will come back from the deeps of the sea,
  The bird from the wilderness back to the tree,
Flowers to the mountain and tides to the shore,
  But he will return to Lochaber no more!

O why should the hills last, that never were young,
  Unperishing stars in the heavens be hung;
Be constant the seasons, undrying the stream,
  And he that was gallant be gone like a dream?
Brave songs will be singing in isles of the West,
  But he will be silent who sang them the best;
The dance will be waiting, the pipes will implore,
  But he will return to Lochaber no more!

Child of the forest! profound is thy sleep,
  The valley that loved thee awakes but to weep;
When our fires are rekindled at dawn of the morn,
  Our griefs burn afresh, and our prayers are forlorn;
The night falls disconsolate, bringing no peace,
  No hope for our dreams, for our sighs no release;
In vain come the true hearts and look from the door,
  For thou wilt return to Lochaber no more!

SIR HENRY NEWBOLT
1862–1938

The Vigil

England! where the sacred flame
    Burns before the inmost shrine,
Where the lips that love thy name
    Consecrate their hopes and thine,
Where the banners of thy dead
Weave their shadows overhead,
Watch beside thine arms tonight,
Pray that God defend the Right.

Think that when tomorrow comes
    War shall claim command of all,
Thou must hear the roll of drums,
    Thou must hear the trumpet's call.
Now, before they silence ruth,
Commune with the voice of truth;
England! on thy knees tonight
Pray that God defend the Right.

Single-hearted, unafraid,
    Hither all thy heroes came,
On this altar's steps were laid
    Gordon's life and Outram's fame.
England! if thy will be yet
By their great example set,
Here beside thine arms tonight
Pray that God defend the Right.

So shalt thou when morning comes
    Rise to conquer or to fall,
Joyful hear the rolling drums,
    Joyful hear the trumpets call,

Then let Memory tell thy heart:
'England! what thou wert, thou art!'
Gird thee with thine ancient might,
Forth! and God defend the Right!

A Letter from the Front

I was out early today, spying about
From the top of a haystack – such a lovely morning –
And when I mounted again to canter back
I saw across a field in the broad sunlight
A young Gunner Subaltern, stalking along
With a rook-rifle held at the ready, and – would you
    believe it? –
A domestic cat, soberly marching beside him.

So I laughed, and felt quite well disposed to the
    youngster,
And shouted out 'the top of the morning' to him,
And wished him 'Good sport!' – and then I remembered
My rank, and his, and what I ought to be doing:
And I rode nearer, and added, 'I can only suppose
You have not seen the Commander-in-Chief's order
Forbidding English officers to annoy their Allies
By hunting and shooting.'
                    But he stood and saluted
And said earnestly, 'I beg your pardon, Sir,
I was only going out to shoot a sparrow
To feed my cat with.'
                    So there was the whole picture,
The lovely early morning, the occasional shell
Screeching and scattering past us, the empty landscape, –
Empty, except for the young Gunner saluting,
And the cat, anxiously watching his every movement.

I may be wrong, and I may have told it badly,
But it struck *me* as being extremely ludicrous.

ROBERT NICHOLS
1893–1944

By the Wood

How still the day is, and the air how bright!
A thrush sings and is silent in the wood;
The hillside sleeps dizzy with heat and light;
A rhythmic murmur fills the quietude;
A woodpecker prolongs his leisured flight,
Rising and falling on the solitude.

But there are those who far from yon wood lie,
Buried within the trench where all were found.
A weight of mould oppresses every eye,
Within that cabin close their limbs are bound,
And there they rot amid the long profound,
Disastrous silence of grey earth and sky.

These once, too, rested where now rests but one,
Who scarce can lift his panged and heavy head,
Who drinks in grief the hot light of the sun,
Whose eyes watch dully the green branches spread,
Who feels his currents ever a slowlier run,
Whose lips repeat a silent ' . . . Dead! all dead!'

O youths to come shall drink air warm and bright,
Shall hear the bird cry in the sunny wood,
All my Young England fell today in fight:
That bird, that wood, was ransomed by our blood!

I pray you when the drum rolls let your mood
Be worthy of our deaths and your delight.

Casualty

They are bringing him down,
He looks at me wanly.
The bandages are brown,
Brown with mud, red only –
But how deep a red! in the breast of the shirt,
Deepening red too, as each whistling breath
Is drawn with the suck of a slow-filling squirt
While waxen cheeks waste to the pallor of death.

O my comrade!
My comrade that you could rest
Your tired body on mine, that your head might be laid
Fallen and heavy – upon this my breast,
That I might take your hands in my hands
To chafe! That abandoned your body might sink
Upon mine, which here helplessly, grievously stands;
That your body might drink
Warmth from my body, strength from my veins,
Life from my heart that monstrously beats,
Beats, beats and strains
After you vainly!
The trench curves. They are gone.
The steep rain teems down.

O my companion!
Who were you? How did you come,
Looking so wanly upon me? I know –
And O, how immensely long I have known –
Those aching eyes, numb face, gradual gloom,
That depth without groan!
Take now my love – this love which alone
I can give you – and shed without pain –
That life if I could I would succour,
Even as it were
This, this, my poor own!

WILFRED OWEN
1893–1918
Killed, Sambre Canal, 4th November

Exposure

Our brains ache, in the merciless iced east winds that
    knive us . . .
Wearied we keep awake because the night is silent . . .
Low, drooping flares confuse our memory of the salient . . .
Worried by silence, sentries whisper, curious, nervous,
              But nothing happens.

Watching, we hear the mad gusts tugging on the wire,
Like twitching agonies of men among its brambles.
Northward, incessantly, the flickering gunnery rumbles,
Far off, like a dull rumour of some other war.
              What are we doing here?

The poignant misery of dawn begins to grow . . .
We only know war lasts, rain soaks, and clouds sag stormy.
Dawn massing in the east her melancholy army
Attacks once more in ranks on shivering ranks of grey,
              But nothing happens.

Sudden successive flights of bullets streak the silence.
Less deadly than the air that shudders black with snow,
With sidelong flowing flakes that flock, pause, and renew,
We watch them wandering up and down the wind's
    nonchalance,
              But nothing happens.

Pale flakes with fingering stealth come feeling for our faces –
We cringe in holes, back on forgotten dreams, and stare,
    snow-dazed,
Deep into grassier ditches. So we drowse, sun-dozed,
Littered with blossoms trickling where the blackbird fusses.
              Is it that we are dying?

Slowly our ghosts drag home: glimpsing the sunk fires,
    glozed
With crusted dark-red jewels; crickets jingle there;
For hours the innocent mice rejoice: the house is theirs;
Shutters and doors, all closed: on us the doors are closed, –
            We turn back to our dying.

Since we believe not otherwise can kind fires burn;
Nor ever suns smile true on child, or field, or fruit.
For God's invincible spring our love is made afraid;
Therefore, not loath, we lie out here; therefore were born,
            For love of God seems dying.

Tonight, His frost will fasten on this mud and us,
Shrivelling many hands, puckering foreheads crisp.
The burying-party, picks and shovels in their shaking grasp
Pause over half-known faces. All their eyes are ice,
            But nothing happens.

The Dead-Beat

He dropped, – more sullenly than wearily,
Lay stupid like a cod, heavy like meat,
And none of us could kick him to his feet;
Just blinked at my revolver, blearily;
 – Didn't appear to know a war was on,
Or see the blasted trench at which he stared.
'I'll do 'em in,' he whined. 'If this hand's spared,
I'll murder them, I will.'
            A low voice said,
'It's Blighty, p'raps, he sees; his pluck's all gone,
Dreaming of all the valiant, that aren't dead:
Bold uncles, smiling ministerially;
Maybe his brave young wife, getting her fun
In some new home, improved materially.
It's not these stiffs have crazed him; nor the Hun.'

We sent him down at last, out of the way.
Unwounded; – stout lad, too, before that strafe.
Malingering? Stretcher-bearers winked, 'Not half.'
Next day I heard the Doc's well-whiskied laugh:
'That scum you sent last night soon died. Hooray!'

Dulce et Decorum Est

Bent double, like old beggars under sacks,
Knock-kneed, coughing like hags, we cursed through
    sludge,
Till on the haunting flares we turned our backs,
And towards our distant rest began to trudge.
Men marched asleep. Many had lost their boots,
But limped on, blood-shod. All went lame, all blind;
Drunk with fatigue; deaf even to the hoots
Of gas-shells dropping softly behind.

Gas! GAS! Quick, boys! – An ecstasy of fumbling,
Fitting the clumsy helmets just in time,
But someone still was yelling out and stumbling
And floundering like a man in fire or lime. –
Dim through the misty panes and thick green light,
As under a green sea, I saw him drowning.

In all my dreams before my helpless sight
He plunges at me, guttering, choking, drowning.

If in some smothering dreams, you too could pace
Behind the wagon that we flung him in,
And watch the white eyes writhing in his face,
His hanging face, like a devil's sick of sin;
If you could hear, at every jolt, the blood
Come gargling from the froth-corrupted lungs,
Bitter as the cud
Of vile, incurable sores on innocent tongues, –
My friend, you would not tell with such high zest
To children ardent for some desperate glory,
The old Lie: *Dulce et decorum est*
Pro patria mori.

Anthem for Doomed Youth

What passing-bells for these who die as cattle?
   Only the monstrous anger of the guns.
   Only the stuttering rifles' rapid rattle
Can patter out their hasty orisons.
No mockeries for them from prayers or bells,
   Nor any voice of mourning save the choirs, –
The shrill, demented choirs of wailing shells;
   And bugles calling for them from sad shires.

What candles may be held to speed them all?
   Not in the hands of boys, but in their eyes
Shall shine the holy glimmers of good-byes.
   The pallor of girls' brows shall be their pall;
Their flowers the tenderness of silent minds,
And each slow dusk a drawing-down of blinds.

Disabled

He sat in a wheeled chair, waiting for dark,
And shivered in his ghastly suit of grey,
Legless, sewn short at elbow. Through the park
Voices of boys rang saddening like a hymn,
Voices of play and pleasures after day,
Till gathering sleep had mothered them from him.

*   *   *

About this time Town used to swing so gay
When glow-lamps budded in the light blue trees,
And girls glanced lovelier as the air grew dim, –
In the old times, before he threw away his knees.

Now he will never feel again how slim
Girls' waists are, or how warm their subtle hands;
All of them touch him like some queer disease.

*   *   *

There was an artist silly for his face,
For it was younger than his youth, last year.
Now, he is old; his back will never brace;
He's lost his colour very far from here,
Poured it down shell-holes till the veins ran dry,
And half his lifetime lapsed in the hot race,
And leap of purple spurted from his thigh.

*   *   *

One time he liked a blood-smear down his leg,
After the matches, carried shoulder-high.
It was after football, when he'd drunk a peg,
He thought he'd better join. – He wonders why.
Someone had said he'd look a god in kilts,
That's why; and may be, too, to please his Meg;
Aye, that was it, to please the giddy jilts
He asked to join. He didn't have to beg;

Smiling they wrote his lie; aged nineteen years.
Germans he scarcely thought of; all their guilt,
And Austria's, did not move him. And no fears
Of Fear came yet. He thought of jewelled hilts
For daggers in plaid socks; of smart salutes;
And care of arms; and leave; and pay arrears;
Esprit de corps; and hints for young recruits.
And soon he was drafted out with drums and cheers.

*   *   *

Some cheered him home, but not as crowds cheer
          Goal.
Only a solemn man who brought him fruits
Thanked him; and then inquired about his soul.

Now, he will spend a few sick years in Institutes,
And do what things the rules consider wise,
And take whatever pity they may dole.
Tonight he noticed how the women's eyes
Passed from him to the strong men that were whole.
How cold and late it is! Why don't they come
And put him into bed? Why don't they come?

Miners

There was a whispering in my hearth,
    A sigh of the coal,
Grown wistful of a former earth
    It might recall.

I listened for a tale of leaves
    And smothered ferns;
Frond-forests; and the low, sly lives
    Before the fawns.

My fire might show steam-phantoms simmer
    From Time's old cauldron,
Before the birds made nests in summer,
    Or men had children.

But the coals were murmuring of their mine,
    And moans down there
Of boys that slept wry sleep, and men
    Writhing for air.

And I saw white bones in the cinder-shard.
    Bones without number;
For many hearts with coal are charred
    And few remember.

I thought of some who worked dark pits
    Of war, and died
Digging the rock where Death reputes
    Peace lies indeed.

Comforted years will sit soft-chaired
    In rooms of amber;
The years will stretch their hands, well-cheered
    By our lives' ember.

The centuries will burn rich loads
    With which we groaned,
Whose warmth shall lull their dreaming lids
    While songs are crooned.
But they will not dream of us poor lads
    Lost in the ground.

Apologia pro Poemate Meo

I, too, saw God through mud, –
    The mud that cracked on cheeks when wretches
    smiled.
    War brought more glory to their eyes than blood,
    And gave their laugh more glee than shakes a child.

Merry it was to laugh there –
    Where death becomes absurd and life absurder.
    For power was on us as we slashed bones bare
    Not to feel sickness or remorse of murder.

I, too, have dropped off fear –
    Behind the barrage, dead as my platoon,
    And sailed my spirit surging, light and clear
    Past the entanglement where hopes lay strewn;

And witnessed exultation –
    Faces that used to curse me, scowl for scowl,
    Shine and lift up with passion of oblation,
    Seraphic for an hour; though they were foul.

I have made fellowships –
    Untold of happy lovers in old song.
    For love is not the binding of fair lips
    With the soft silk of eyes that look and long,

By Joy, whose ribbon slips, –
    But wound with war's hard wire whose stakes are
      strong;
    Bound with the bandage of the arm that drips;
    Knit in the webbing of the rifle-thong.

I have perceived much beauty
    In the hoarse oaths that kept our courage straight;
    Heard music in the silentness of duty;
    Found peace where shell-storms spouted reddest spate.

Nevertheless, except you share
    With them in hell the sorrowful dark of hell,
    Whose world is but the trembling of a flare,
    And heaven but as the highway for a shell,

You shall not hear their mirth:
    You shall not come to think them well content
    By any jest of mine. These men are worth
    Your tears. You are not worth their merriment.

The Show

> We have fallen in the dreams the ever-living
> Breathe on the tarnished mirror of the world,
> And then smooth out with ivory hands and sigh.
>
> W. B. YEATS

My soul looked down from a vague height with Death,
As unremembering how I rose or why,
And saw a sad land, weak with sweats of dearth,
Grey, cratered like the moon with hollow woe,
And pitted with great pocks and scabs of plagues.

Across its beard, that horror of harsh wire,
There moved thin caterpillars, slowly uncoiled.
It seemed they pushed themselves to be as plugs
Of ditches, where they writhed and shrivelled, killed.

By them had slimy paths been trailed and scraped
Round myriad warts that might be little hills.

From gloom's last dregs these long-strung creatures crept,
And vanished out of dawn down hidden holes.

(And smell came up from those foul openings
As out of mouths, or deep wounds deepening.)

On dithering feet upgathered, more and more,
Brown strings, towards strings of grey, with bristling
    spines,
All migrants from green fields, intent on mire.

Those that were grey, of more abundant spawns,
Ramped on the rest and ate them and were eaten.

I saw their bitten backs curve, loop, and straighten,
I watched those agonies curl, lift, and flatten.

Whereat, in terror what that sight might mean,
I reeled and shivered earthward like a feather.

And Death fell with me, like a deepening moan.
And He, picking a manner of worm, which half had hid
Its bruises in the earth, but crawled no further,
Showed me its feet, the feet of many men,
And the fresh-severed head of it, my head.

Insensibility

1

Happy are men who yet before they are killed
Can let their veins run cold.
Whom no compassion fleers
Or makes their feet
Sore on the alleys cobbled with their brothers.
The front line withers,
But they are troops who fade, not flowers
For poets' tearful fooling:
Men, gaps for filling:
Losses who might have fought
Longer; but no one bothers.

2

And some cease feeling
Even themselves or for themselves.
Dullness best solves
The tease and doubt of shelling,
And Chance's strange arithmetic
Comes simpler than the reckoning of their shilling.
They keep no check on armies' decimation.

3

Happy are these who lose imagination:
They have enough to carry with ammunition.
Their spirit drags no pack,

Their old wounds save with cold can not more ache.
Having seen all things red,
Their eyes are rid
Of the hurt of the colour of blood for ever.

The Send-off

Down the close, darkening lanes they sang their way
To the siding-shed,
And lined the train with faces grimly gay.

Their breasts were stuck all white with wreath and spray
As men's are, dead.

Dull porters watched them, and a casual tramp
Stood staring hard,
Sorry to miss them from the upland camp.
Then, unmoved, signals nodded, and a lamp
Winked to the guard.

So secretly, like wrongs hushed-up, they went.
They were not ours:
We never heard to which front these were sent.

Nor there if they yet mock what women meant
Who gave them flowers.

Shall they return to beatings of great bells
In wild train-loads?
A few, a few, too few for drums and yells,
May creep back, silent, to village wells
Up half-known roads.

Mental Cases

Who are these? Why sit they here in twilight?
Wherefore rock they, purgatorial shadows,
Drooping tongues from jaws that slob their relish,
Baring teeth that leer like skulls' teeth wicked?
Stroke on stroke of pain, – but what slow panic,
Gouged these chasms round their fretted sockets?
Ever from their hair and through their hands' palms
Misery swelters. Surely we have perished
Sleeping, and walk hell; but who these hellish?

  – These are men whose minds the Dead have ravished.
Memory fingers in their hair of murders,
Multitudinous murders they once witnessed.
Wading sloughs of flesh these helpless wander,
Treading blood from lungs that had loved laughter.
Always they must see these things and hear them,
Batter of guns and shatter of flying muscles,
Carnage incomparable, and human squander,
Rucked too thick for these men's extrication.

Therefore still their eyeballs shrink tormented
Back into their brains, because on their sense
Sunlight seems a blood-smear; night comes blood-black;
Dawn breaks open like a wound that bleeds afresh.
  – Thus their heads wear this hilarious, hideous,
Awful falseness of set-smiling corpses.
  – Thus their hands are plucking at each other;
Picking at the rope-knouts of their scourging;
Snatching after us who smote them, brother,
Pawing us who dealt them war and madness.

Futility

Move him into the sun –
Gently its touch awoke him once,
At home, whispering of fields unsown.
Always it woke him, even in France,
Until this morning and this snow.
If anything might rouse him now
The kind old sun will know.

Think how it wakes the seeds, –
Woke, once, the clays of a cold star.
Are limbs, so dear-achieved, are sides,
Full-nerved – still warm – too hard to stir?
Was it for this the clay grew tall?
 – O what made fatuous sunbeams toil
To break earth's sleep at all?

Strange Meeting

It seemed that out of battle I escaped
Down some profound dull tunnel, long since scooped
Through granites which titanic wars had groined.
Yet also there encumbered sleepers groaned,
Too fast in thought or death to be bestirred.
Then, as I probed them, one sprang up, and stared
With piteous recognition in fixed eyes,
Lifting distressful hands as if to bless.
And by his smile, I knew that sullen hall,
By his dead smile I knew we stood in Hell.
With a thousand pains that vision's face was grained;
Yet no blood reached there from the upper ground,
And no guns thumped, or down the flues made moan.
'Strange friend,' I said, 'here is no cause to mourn.'
'None,' said the other, 'save the undone years,

The hopelessness. Whatever hope is yours,
Was my life also; I went hunting wild
After the wildest beauty in the world,
Which lies not calm in eyes, or braided hair,
But mocks the steady running of the hour,
And if it grieves, grieves richlier than here.
For by my glee might many men have laughed,
And of my weeping something had been left,
Which must die now. I mean the truth untold,
The pity of war, the pity war distilled.
Now men will go content with what we spoiled.
Or, discontent, boil bloody, and be spilled.
They will be swift with swiftness of the tigress,
None will break ranks, though nations trek from progress.
Courage was mine, and I had mystery,
Wisdom was mine, and I had mastery;
To miss the march of this retreating world
Into vain citadels that are not walled.
Then, when much blood had clogged their chariot-wheels
I would go up and wash them from sweet wells,
Even with truths that lie too deep for taint.
I would have poured my spirit without stint
But not through wounds; not on the cess of war.
Foreheads of men have bled where no wounds were.
I am the enemy you killed, my friend.
I knew you in this dark; for so you frowned
Yesterday through me as you jabbed and killed.
I parried; but my hands were loath and cold.
Let us sleep now . . . '

The Sentry

We'd found an old Boche dug-out, and he knew,
And gave us hell, for shell on frantic shell
Hammered on top, but never quite burst through.
Rain, guttering down in waterfalls of slime
Kept slush waist-high that, rising hour by hour,
Choked up the steps too thick with clay to climb.
What murk of air remained stank old, and sour
With fumes of whizz-bangs, and the smell of men
Who'd lived there years, and left their curse in the den,
If not their corpses . . .
                              There we herded from the blast
Of whizz-bangs, but one found our door at last, –
Buffeting eyes and breath, snuffing the candles.
And thud! flump! thud! down the steep steps came
      thumping
And splashing in the flood, deluging muck –
The sentry's body; then, his rifle, handles
Of old Boche bombs, and mud in ruck on ruck.
We dredged him up, for killed, until he whined
'O sir, my eyes – I'm blind – I'm blind, I'm blind!'
Coaxing, I held a flame against his lids
And said if he could see the least blurred light
He was not blind; in time he'd get all right.
'I can't,' he sobbed. Eyeballs, huge-bulged like squids',
Watch my dreams still; but I forgot him there
In posting next for duty, and sending a scout
To beg a stretcher somewhere, and floundering about
To other posts under the shrieking air.

                    *   *   *

Those other wretches, how they bled and spewed,
And one who would have drowned himself for good, –
I try not to remember these things now.
Let dread hark back for one word only: how
Half listening to that sentry's moans and jumps,
And the wild chattering of his broken teeth,

Renewed most horribly whenever crumps
Pummelled the roof and slogged the air beneath –
Through the dense din, I say, we heard him shout
'I see your lights!' But ours had long died out.

Smile, Smile, Smile

Head to limp head, the sunk-eyed wounded scanned
Yesterday's *Mail*; the casualties (typed small)
And (large) Vast Booty from our Latest Haul.
Also, they read of Cheap Homes, not yet planned
For, said the paper, 'When this war is done
The men's first instinct will be making homes.
Meanwhile their foremost need is aerodromes,
It being certain war has but begun.
Peace would do wrong to our undying dead, –
The sons we offered might regret they died
If we got nothing lasting in their stead.
We must be solidly indemnified.
Though all be worthy Victory which all bought,
We rulers sitting in this ancient spot
Would wrong our very selves if we forgot
The greatest glory will be theirs who fought,
Who kept this nation in integrity.'
Nation? – The half-limbed readers did not chafe
But smiled at one another curiously
Like secret men who know their secret safe.
(This is the thing they know and never speak,
That England one by one had fled to France,
Not many elsewhere now save under France.)
Pictures of these broad smiles appear each week,
And people in whose voice real feeling rings
Say: How they smile! They're happy now, poor things.

Spring Offensive

Halted against the shade of a last hill,
They fed, and, lying easy, were at ease
And, finding comfortable chests and knees,
Carelessly slept. But many there stood still
To face the stark, blank sky beyond the ridge,
Knowing their feet had come to the end of the world.

Marvelling they stood, and watched the long grass swirled
By the May breeze, murmurous with wasp and midge,
For though the summer oozed into their veins
Like an injected drug for their bodies' pains,
Sharp on their souls hung the imminent line of grass,
Fearfully flashed the sky's mysterious glass.

Hour after hour they ponder the warm field –
And the far valley behind, where the buttercup
Had blessed with gold their slow boots coming up,
Where even the little brambles would not yield,
But clutched and clung to them like sorrowing hands;
They breathe like trees unstirred.

Till like a cold gust thrills the little word
At which each body and its soul begird
And tighten them for battle. No alarms
Of bugles, no high flags, no clamorous haste –
Only a lift and flare of eyes that faced
The sun, like a friend with whom their love is done.
O larger shone that smile against the sun, –
Mightier than his whose bounty these have spurned.

So, soon they topped the hill, and raced together
Over an open stretch of herb and heather
Exposed. And instantly the whole sky burned
With fury against them; earth set sudden cups
In thousands for their blood; and the green slope
Chasmed and steepened sheer to infinite space.

Of them who running on that last high place
Leapt to swift unseen bullets, or went up
On the hot blast and fury of hell's upsurge,
Or plunged and fell away past this world's verge,
Some say God caught them even before they fell.

But what say such as from existence' brink
Ventured but drave too swift to sink,
The few who rushed in the body to enter hell,
And there out-fiending all its fiends and flames
With superhuman inhumanities,
Long-famous glories, immemorial shames –
And crawling slowly back, have by degrees
Regained cool peaceful air in wonder –
Why speak not they of comrades that went under?

The Chances

I mind as 'ow the night afore that show
Us five got talkin', – we was in the know.
'Over the top tomorrer; boys, we're for it.
First wave we are, first ruddy wave; that's tore it!'
'Ah well,' says Jimmy, – an' 'e's seen some scrappin' –
'There ain't no more nor five things 'as can 'appen:
Ye get knocked out; else wounded – bad or cushy;
Scuppered; or nowt except yer feelin' mushy.'
One of us got the knock-out, blown to chops.
T'other was 'urt, like, losin' both 'is props.
An' one, to use the word of 'ypocrites,
'Ad the misfortoon to be took be Fritz.
Now me, I wasn't scratched, praise God Almighty,
(Though next time please I'll thank 'im for a blighty).
But poor young Jim, 'e's livin' an' 'e's not;
'E reckoned 'e'd five chances, an' 'e 'ad;
'Es wounded, killed, and pris'ner, all the lot,
The bloody lot all rolled in one. Jim's mad.

EDGELL RICKWORD
1898–1982

The Soldier Addresses His Body

I shall be mad if you get smashed about,
we've had good times together, you and I;
although you groused a bit when luck was out,
say a girl turned us down, or we went dry.

But there's a world of things we haven't done,
countries not seen, where people do strange things;
eat fish alive, and mimic in the sun
the solemn gestures of their stone-grey kings.

I've heard of forests that are dim at noon
where snakes and creepers wrestle all day long;
where vivid beasts grow pale with the full moon,
gibber and cry, and wail a mad old song;

because at the full moon the Hippogriff
with crinkled ivory snout and agate feet,
with his green eye will glare them cold and stiff
for the coward Wyvern to come down and eat.

Vodka and kvass, and bitter mountain wines
we've never drunk; nor snatched the bursting grapes
to pelt slim girls among Sicilian vines,
who'd flicker through the leaves, faint frolic shapes.

Yes, there's a world of things we've never done,
but it's a sweat to knock them into rhyme,
let's have a drink, and give the cards a run
and leave dull verse to the dull peaceful time.

Winter Warfare

Colonel Cold strode up the Line
   (tabs of rime and spurs of ice);
stiffened all that met his glare:
   horses, men, and lice.

Visited a forward post,
   left them burning, ear to foot;
fingers stuck to biting steel,
   toes to frozen boot.

Stalked on into No Man's Land,
   turned the wire to fleecy wool,
iron stakes to sugar sticks
   snapping at a pull.

Those who watched with hoary eyes
   saw two figures gleaming there;
Hauptmann Kälte, Colonel Cold,
   gaunt in the grey air.

Stiffly, tinkling spurs they moved,
   glassy-eyed, with glinting heel
stabbing those who lingered there
   torn by screaming steel.

ISAAC ROSENBERG

1890–1918
Killed, Arras, 1st April

Marching

As Seen from the Left File

My eyes catch ruddy necks
Sturdily pressed back –
All a red brick moving glint.
Like flaming pendulums, hands
Swing across the khaki –
Mustard-coloured khaki –
To the automatic feet.

We husband the ancient glory
In these bared necks and hands.
Not broke is the forge of Mars;
But a subtler brain beats iron
To shoe the hoofs of death
(Who paws dynamic air now).
Blind fingers loose an iron cloud
To rain immortal darkness
On strong eyes.

Break of Day in the Trenches

The darkness crumbles away –
It is the same old druid Time as ever.
Only a live thing leaps my hand –
A queer sardonic rat –
As I pull the parapet's poppy

To stick behind my ear.
Droll rat, they would shoot you if they knew
Your cosmopolitan sympathies.
Now you have touched this English hand
You will do the same to a German –
Soon, no doubt, if it be your pleasure
To cross the sleeping green between.
It seems you inwardly grin as you pass
Strong eyes, fine limbs, haughty athletes
Less chanced than you for life,
Bonds to the whims of murder,
Sprawled in the bowels of the earth,
The torn fields of France.
What do you see in our eyes
At the shrieking iron and flame
Hurled through still heavens?
What quaver – what heart aghast?
Poppies whose roots are in man's veins
Drop, and are ever dropping;
But mine in my ear is safe,
Just a little white with the dust.

Louse Hunting

Nudes – stark and glistening,
Yelling in lurid glee. Grinning faces
And raging limbs
Whirl over the floor one fire.
For a shirt verminously busy
Yon soldier tore from his throat, with oaths
Godhead might shrink at, but not the lice.
And soon the shirt was aflare
Over the candle he'd lit while we lay.

Then we all sprang up and stript
To hunt the verminous brood.

Soon like a demons' pantomime
The place was raging.
See the silhouettes agape,
See the gibbering shadows
Mixed with the battled arms on the wall.
See gargantuan hooked fingers
Pluck in supreme flesh
To smutch supreme littleness.
See the merry limbs in hot Highland fling
Because some wizard vermin
Charmed from the quiet this revel
When our ears were half lulled
By the dark music
Blown from Sleep's trumpet.

Returning, We Hear the Larks

Sombre the night is.
And though we have our lives, we know
What sinister threat lurks there.

Dragging these anguished limbs, we only know
This poison-blasted track opens on our camp —
On a little safe sleep.

But hark! joy — joy — strange joy.
Lo! heights of night ringing with unseen larks.
Music showering on our upturned list'ning faces.

Death could drop from the dark
As easily as song —
But song only dropped,
Like a blind man's dreams on the sand
By dangerous tides,
Like a girl's dark hair for she dreams no ruin lies
    there,
Or her kisses where a serpent hides.

Dead Man's Dump

The plunging limbers over the shattered track
Racketed with their rusty freight,
Stuck out like many crowns of thorns,
And the rusty stakes like sceptres old
To stay the flood of brutish men
Upon our brothers dear.

The wheels lurched over sprawled dead
But pained them not, though their bones crunched,
Their shut mouths made no moan.
They lie there huddled, friend and foeman,
Man born of man, and born of woman,
And shells go crying over them
From night till night and now.

Earth has waited for them,
All the time of their growth
Fretting for their decay:
Now she has them at last!
In the strength of their strength
Suspended – stopped and held.

What fierce imaginings their dark souls lit?
Earth! have they gone into you!
Somewhere they must have gone,
And flung on your hard back
Is their soul's sack
Emptied of God-ancestralled essences.
Who hurled them out? Who hurled?

None saw their spirits' shadow shake the grass,
Or stood aside for the half used life to pass
Out of those doomed nostrils and the doomed mouth,
When the swift iron burning bee
Drained the wild honey of their youth.

What of us who, flung on the shrieking pyre,
Walk, our usual thoughts untouched,
Our lucky limbs as on ichor fed,
Immortal seeming ever?
Perhaps when the flames beat loud on us,
A fear may choke in our veins
And the startled blood may stop.

The air is loud with death,
The dark air spurts with fire,
The explosions ceaseless are.
Timelessly now, some minutes past,
These dead strode time with vigorous life,
Till the shrapnel called 'An end!'
But not to all. In bleeding pangs
Some borne on stretchers dreamed of home,
Dear things, war-blotted from their hearts.

Maniac Earth! howling and flying, your bowel
Seared by the jagged fire, the iron love,
The impetuous storm of savage love.
Dark Earth! dark Heavens! swinging in chemic smoke,
What dead are born when you kiss each soundless
     soul
With lightning and thunder from your mined heart,
Which man's self dug, and his blind fingers loosed?

A man's brains splattered on
A stretcher-bearer's face;
His shook shoulders slipped their load,
But when they bent to look again
The drowning soul was sunk too deep
For human tenderness.

They left this dead with the older dead,
Stretched at the cross roads.

Burnt black by strange decay
Their sinister faces lie,
The lid over each eye,

The grass and coloured clay
More motion have than they,
Joined to the great sunk silences.

Here is one not long dead;
His dark hearing caught our far wheels,
And the choked soul stretched weak hands
To reach the living word the far wheels said,
The blood-dazed intelligence beating for light,
Crying through the suspense of the far torturing
    wheels
Swift for the end to break
Or the wheels to break,
Cried as the tide of the world broke over his sight.

Will they come? Will they ever come?
Even as the mixed hoofs of the mules,
The quivering-bellied mules,
And the rushing wheels all mixed
With his tortured upturned sight.
So we crashed round the bend,
We heard his weak scream,
We heard his very last sound,
And our wheels grazed his dead face.

Daughters of War

Space beats the ruddy freedom of their limbs –
Their naked dances with man's spirit naked
By the root side of the tree of life
(The under side of things
And shut from earth's profoundest eyes).

I saw in prophetic gleams
These mighty daughters in their dances
Beckon each soul aghast from its crimson corpse
To mix in their glittering dances.

I heard the mighty daughters' giant sighs
In sleepless passion for the sons of valour,
And envy of the days of flesh
Barring their love with mortal boughs across –
The mortal boughs, the mortal tree of life.
The old bark burnt with iron wars
They blow to a live flame
To char the young green days
And reach the occult soul; they have no softer lure –
No softer lure than the savage ways of death.
We were satisfied of our lords the moon and the sun
To take our wage of sleep and bread and warmth –
These maidens came – these strong everliving
    Amazons,
And in an easy might their wrists
Of night's sway and noon's sway the sceptres brake,
Clouding the wild – the soft lustres of our eyes.

Clouding the wild lustres, the clinging tender lights;
Driving the darkness into the flame of day
With the Amazonian wind of them
Over our corroding faces
That must be broken – broken for evermore
So the soul can leap out
Into their huge embraces.
Though there are human faces
Best sculptures of Deity,
And sinews lusted after
By the Archangels tall,
Even these must leap to the love-heat of these
    maidens
From the flame of terrene days,
Leaving grey ashes to the wind – to the wind.

One (whose great lifted face,
Where wisdom's strength and beauty's strength
And the thewed strength of large beasts
Moved and merged, gloomed and lit)
Was speaking, surely, as the earth-men's earth fell
    away;

Whose new hearing drank the sound
Where pictures lutes and mountains mixed
With the loosed spirit of a thought.
Essenced to language, thus –

'My sisters force their males
From the doomed earth, from the doomed glee
And hankering of hearts.
Frail hands gleam up through the human quagmire
    and lips of ash
Seem to wail, as in sad faded paintings
Far sunken and strange.
My sisters have their males
Clean of the dust of old days
That clings about those white hands
And yearns in those voices sad.
But these shall not see them,
Or think of them in any days or years;
They are my sisters' lovers in other days and years.'

Girl to Soldier on Leave

I love you – Titan lover,
My own storm-days' Titan.
Greater than the son of Zeus,
I know whom I would choose.

Titan – my splendid rebel –
The old Prometheus
Wanes like a ghost before your power –
His pangs were joys to yours.

Pallid days arid and wan
Tied your soul fast.
Babel-cities' smoky tops
Pressed upon your growth

Weary gyves. What were you
But a word in the brain's ways,
Or the sleep of Circe's swine?
One gyve holds you yet.

It held you hiddenly on the Somme
Tied from my heart at home.
O must it loosen now? I wish
You were bound with the old old gyves.

Love! you love me – your eyes
Have looked through death at mine.
You have tempted a grave too much.
I let you – I repine.

The Destruction of Jerusalem
by the Babylonian Hordes

They left their Babylon bare
Of all its tall men,
Of all its proud horses;
They made for Lebanon.

And shadowy sowers went
Before their spears to sow
The fruit whose taste is ash
For Judah's soul to know.

They who bowed to the Bull god
Whose wings roofed Babylon,
In endless hosts darkened
The bright-heavened Lebanon.

They washed their grime in pools
Where laughing girls forgot
The wiles they used for Solomon.
Sweet laughter! remembered not.

Sweet laughter charred in the flame
That clutched the cloud and earth
While Solomon's towers crashed between,
The gird of Babylon's mirth.

The Immortals

I killed them, but they would not die.
Yea! all the day and all the night
For them I could not rest nor sleep,
Nor guard from them nor hide in flight.

Then in my agony I turned
And made my hands red in their gore.
In vain – for faster than I slew
They rose more cruel than before.

I killed and killed with slaughter mad;
I killed till all my strength was gone.
And still they rose to torture me,
For Devils only die for fun.

I used to think the Devil hid
In women's smiles and wine's carouse.
I called him Satan, Balzebub.
But now I call him dirty louse.

SAKI (H. H. MUNRO)

1870–1916
Killed, the Somme, 14th November

Carol

While shepherds watched their flocks by night
  All seated on the ground,
A high-explosive shell came down
  And mutton rained around.

SIEGFRIED SASSOON
1886–1967

The Death-Bed

He drowsed and was aware of silence heaped
Round him, unshaken as the steadfast walls;
Aqueous like floating rays of amber light,
Soaring and quivering in the wings of sleep,
Silence and safety; and his mortal shore
Lipped by the inward moonless waves of death.

Someone was holding water to his mouth.
He swallowed, unresisting; moaned and dropped
Through crimson gloom to darkness; and forgot
The opiate throb and ache that was his wound.
Water – calm, sliding green above the weir;
Water – a sky-lit alley for his boat,
Bird-voiced, and bordered with reflected flowers
And shaken hues of summer: drifting down,
He dipped contented oars, and sighed, and slept.

Night, with a gust of wind, was in the ward,
Blowing the curtain to a glimmering curve.
Night. He was blind; he could not see the stars
Glinting among the wraiths of wandering cloud;
Queer blots of colour, purple, scarlet, green,
Flickered and faded in his drowning eyes.

Rain; he could hear it rustling through the dark;
Fragrance and passionless music woven as one;
Warm rain on drooping roses; pattering showers
That soak the woods; not the harsh rain that sweeps
Behind the thunder, but a trickling peace
Gently and slowly washing life away.

*   *   *

He stirred, shifting his body; then the pain
Leaped like a prowling beast, and gripped and tore
His groping dreams with grinding claws and fangs.
But someone was beside him; soon he lay
Shuddering because that evil thing had passed.
And Death, who'd stepped toward him, paused and
    stared.

Light many lamps and gather round his bed.
Lend him your eyes, warm blood, and will to live.
Speak to him; rouse him; you may save him yet.
He's young; he hated war; how should he die
When cruel old campaigners win safe through?

But Death replied: 'I choose him.' So he went,
And there was silence in the summer night;
Silence and safety; and the veils of sleep.
Then, far away, the thudding of the guns.

They

The Bishop tells us: 'When the boys come back
They will not be the same; for they'll have fought
In a just cause: they lead the last attack
On Anti-Christ; their comrades' blood has bought
New right to breed an honourable race.
They have challenged Death and dared him face to
    face.'

'We're none of us the same!' the boys reply.
'For George lost both his legs; and Bill's stone blind;
Poor Jim's shot through the lungs and like to die;
And Bert's gone syphilitic: you'll not find
A chap who's served that hasn't found *some* change.'
And the Bishop said: 'The ways of God are strange!'

Base Details

If I were fierce and bald and short of breath,
   I'd live with scarlet Majors at the Base,
And speed glum heroes up the line to death.
   You'd see me with my puffy petulant face,
Guzzling and gulping in the best hotel,
   Reading the Roll of Honour. 'Poor young chap,'
I'd say – 'I used to know his father well;
   Yes, we've lost heavily in this last scrap.'
And when the war is done and youth stone dead
I'd toddle safely home and die – in bed.

The General

'Good-morning; good-morning!' the General said
When we met him last week on our way to the Line.
Now the soldiers he smiled at are most of 'em dead,
And we're cursing his staff for incompetent swine.
'He's a cheery old card,' grunted Harry to Jack
As they slogged up to Arras with rifle and pack.

*   *   *

But he did for them both by his plan of attack.

Dreamers

Soldiers are citizens of death's grey land,
  Drawing no dividend from time's tomorrows.
In the great hour of destiny they stand,
  Each with his feuds and jealousies and sorrows.
Soldiers are sworn to action; they must win
  Some flaming fatal climax with their lives.
Soldiers are dreamers; when the guns begin
  They think of firelit homes, clean beds, and wives.

I see them in foul dug-outs, gnawed by rats,
  And in the ruined trenches, lashed with rain,
Dreaming of things they did with balls and bats,
  And mocked by hopeless longing to regain
Bank-holidays, and picture-shows, and spats,
  And going to the office in the train.

A Working Party

Three hours ago he blundered up the trench,
Sliding and poising, groping with his boots;
Sometimes he tripped and lurched against the walls
With hands that pawed the sodden bags of chalk.
He couldn't see the man who walked in front;
Only he heard the drum and rattle of feet
Stepping along barred trench boards, often splashing
Wretchedly where the sludge was ankle-deep.

Voices would grunt 'Keep to your right – make way!'
When squeezing past some men from the front-line:
White faces peered, puffing a point of red;
Candles and braziers glinted through the chinks
And curtain-flaps of dug-outs; then the gloom
Swallowed his sense of sight; he stooped and swore
Because a sagging wire had caught his neck.

A flare went up; the shining whiteness spread
And flickered upward, showing nimble rats
And mounds of glimmering sand-bags, bleached with
    rain;
Then the slow silver moment died in dark.
The wind came posting by with chilly gusts
And buffeting at corners, piping thin.
And dreary through the crannies; rifle-shots
Would split and crack and sing along the night,
And shells came calmly through the drizzling air
To burst with hollow bang below the hill.
Three hours ago he stumbled up the trench;
Now he will never walk that road again:
He must be carried back, a jolting lump
Beyond all need of tenderness and care.

He was a young man with a meagre wife
And two small children in a Midland town;
He showed their photographs to all his mates,
And they considered him a decent chap
Who did his work and hadn't much to say,
And always laughed at other people's jokes
Because he hadn't any of his own.

That night when he was busy at his job
Of piling bags along the parapet,
He thought how slow time went, stamping his feet
And blowing on his fingers, pinched with cold.
He thought of getting back by half-past twelve,
And tot of rum to send him warm to sleep
In draughty dug-out frowsty with the fumes
Of coke, and full of snoring weary men.

He pushed another bag along the top,
Craning his body outward; then a flare
Gave one white glimpse of No Man's Land and wire;
And as he dropped his head the instant split
His startled life with lead, and all went out.

Attack

At dawn the ridge emerges massed and dun
In the wild purple of the glowering sun
Smouldering through spouts of drifting smoke that
    shroud
The menacing scarred slope; and, one by one,
Tanks creep and topple forward to the wire.
The barrage roars and lifts. Then, clumsily bowed
With bombs and guns and shovels and battle-gear,
Men jostle and climb to meet the bristling fire.
Lines of grey, muttering faces, masked with fear,
They leave their trenches, going over the top,
While time ticks blank and busy on their wrists,
And hope, with furtive eyes and grappling fists,
Flounders in mud. O Jesu, make it stop!

Counter-Attack

We'd gained our first objective hours before
While dawn broke like a face with blinking eyes,
Pallid, unshaved and thirsty, blind with smoke.
Things seemed all right at first. We held their line,
With bombers posted, Lewis guns well placed,
And clink of shovels deepening the shallow trench.
    The place was rotten with dead; green clumsy legs
    High-booted, sprawled and grovelled along the saps
    And trunks, face downward, in the sucking mud,
    Wallowed like trodden sand-bags loosely filled;
    And naked sodden buttocks, mats of hair,
    Bulged, clotted heads slept in the plastering slime.
    And then the rain began, – the jolly old rain!

A yawning soldier knelt against the bank,
Staring across the morning blear with fog;
He wondered when the Allemands would get busy;
And then, of course, they started with five-nines
Traversing, sure as fate, and never a dud.
Mute in the clamour of shells he watched them burst
Spouting dark earth and wire with gusts from hell,
While posturing giants dissolved in drifts of smoke.
He crouched and flinched, dizzy with galloping fear,
Sick for escape, – loathing the strangled horror
And butchered, frantic gestures of the dead.

An officer came blundering down the trench:
'Stand-to and man the fire-step!' On he went . . .
Gasping and bawling, 'Fire-step . . . counter-attack!'

   Then the haze lifted. Bombing on the right
   Down the old sap: machine-guns on the left;
   And stumbling figures looming out in front.
   'O Christ, they're coming at us!' Bullets spat,
And he remembered his rifle . . . rapid fire . . .
And started blazing wildly . . . then a bang
Crumpled and spun him sideways, knocked him out
To grunt and wriggle: none heeded him; he choked
And fought the flapping veils of smothering gloom,
Lost in a blurred confusion of yells and groans . . .
Down, and down, and down, he sank and drowned,
Bleeding to death. The counter-attack had failed.

The Rearguard

Hindenburg Line, April 1917

Groping along the tunnel, step by step,
He winked his prying torch with patching glare
From side to side, and sniffed the unwholesome air.
Tins, boxes, bottles, shapes too vague to know,
A mirror smashed, the mattress from a bed;
And he, exploring fifty feet below
The rosy gloom of battle overhead.

Tripping, he grabbed the wall; saw someone lie
Humped at his feet, half-hidden by a rug,
And stooped to give the sleeper's arm a tug.
'I'm looking for headquarters.' No reply.
'God blast your neck!' (For days he'd had no sleep,)
'Get up and guide me through this stinking place.'
Savage, he kicked a soft, unanswering heap,
And flashed his beam across the livid face
Terribly glaring up, whose eyes yet wore
Agony dying hard ten days before;
And fists of fingers clutched a blackening wound.

Alone he staggered on until he found
Dawn's ghost that filtered down a shafted stair
To the dazed, muttering creatures underground
Who hear the boom of shells in muffled sound.
At last, with sweat of horror in his hair,
He climbed through darkness to the twilight air
Unloading hell behind him step by step.

Glory of Women

You love us when we're heroes, home on leave,
Or wounded in a mentionable place.
You worship decorations; you believe
That chivalry redeems the war's disgrace.
You make us shells. You listen with delight,
By tales of dirt and danger fondly thrilled.
You crown our distant ardours while we fight,
And mourn our laurelled memories when we're killed.
You can't believe that British troops 'retire'
When hell's last horror breaks them, and they run,
Trampling the terrible corpses – blind with blood.
    O German mother dreaming by the fire,
      While you are knitting socks to send your son
      His face is trodden deeper in the mud.

Does It Matter?

Does it matter? – losing your legs? . . .
For people will always be kind,
And you need not show that you mind
When the others come in after football
To gobble their muffins and eggs.

Does it matter? – losing your sight? . . .
There's such splendid work for the blind;
And people will always be kind,
As you sit on the terrace remembering
And turning your face to the light.

Do they matter? – those dreams from the pit? . . .
You can drink and forget and be glad,
And people won't say that you're mad;
For they'll know that you've fought for your country,
And no one will worry a bit.

Suicide in the Trenches

I knew a simple soldier boy
Who grinned at life in empty joy,
Slept soundly through the lonesome dark,
And whistled early with the lark.

In winter trenches, cowed and glum,
With crumps and lice and lack of rum,
He put a bullet through his brain.
No one spoke of him again.

*   *   *

You smug-faced crowds with kindling eye
Who cheer when soldier lads march by,
Sneak home and pray you'll never know
The hell where youth and laughter go.

Memorial Tablet

Great War

Squire nagged and bullied till I went to fight
(Under Lord Derby's scheme). I died in hell –
(They called it Passchendaele); my wound was slight,
And I was hobbling back, and then a shell
Burst slick upon the duck-boards; so I fell
Into the bottomless mud, and lost the light.

In sermon-time, while Squire is in his pew,
He gives my gilded name a thoughtful stare;
For though low down upon the list, I'm there:
'In proud and glorious memory' – that's my due.
Two bleeding years I fought in France for Squire;
I suffered anguish that he's never guessed;
Once I came home on leave; and then went west.
What greater glory could a man desire?

Aftermath

Have you forgotten yet? . . .
For the world's events have rumbled on since those
    gagged days,
Like traffic checked awhile at the crossing of city ways:
And the haunted gap in your mind has filled with
    thoughts that flow
Like clouds in the lit heaven of life; and you're a man
    reprieved to go,
Taking your peaceful share of Time, with joy to spare.
*But the past is just the same, – and War's a bloody
    game* . . .
Have you forgotten yet? . . .
*Look down, and swear by the slain of the War that you'll
    never forget.*

Do you remember the dark months you held the sector at
    Mametz, –
The nights you watched and wired and dug and piled
    sandbags on parapets?
Do you remember the rats; and the stench
Of corpses rotting in front of the front-line trench, –
And dawn coming, dirty-white, and chill with a hopeless
    rain?
Do you ever stop and ask, 'Is it all going to happen
    again?'

Do you remember that hour of din before the attack,
And the anger, the blind compassion that seized and
    shook you then
As you peered at the doomed and haggard faces of your
    men?
Do you remember the stretcher-cases lurching back –
With dying eyes and lolling heads, – those ashen-grey
Masks of the lads who once were keen and kind and gay?

Have you forgotten yet? . . .
*Look up, and swear by the green of the Spring that you'll
    never forget.*

On Passing the New Menin Gate

Who will remember, passing through this Gate,
The unheroic Dead who fed the guns?
Who shall absolve the foulness of their fate, –
Those doomed, conscripted, unvictorious ones?
   Crudely renewed, the Salient holds its own.
   Paid are its dim defenders by this pomp;
   Paid, with a pile of peace-complacent stone,
   The armies who endured that sullen swamp.

Here was the world's worst wound. And here with pride,
'Their name liveth for ever,' the Gateway claims.
Was ever an immolation so belied
As these intolerably nameless names?
Well might the Dead who struggled in the slime
Rise and deride this sepulchre of crime.

Wirers

'Pass it along, the wiring party's going out' –
And yawning sentries mumble, 'Wirers going out.'
Unravelling; twisting; hammering stakes with muffled
    thud,
They toil with stealthy haste and anger in their blood.

The Boche sends up a flare. Black forms stand rigid there
Stock-still like posts; then darkness, and the clumsy
    ghosts
Stride thither and thither, whispering, tripped by
    clutching snare
Of snags and tangles.
               Ghastly dawn with vaporous coasts
Gleams desolate along the sky, night's misery ended.

Young Hughes was badly hit; I heard him carried away,
Moaning at every lurch; no doubt he'll die today.
But *we* can say the front-line wire's been safely mended.

ALAN SEEGER

1888–1916
Killed, the Somme, 4th July

Rendezvous

I have a rendezvous with Death
At some disputed barricade,
When Spring comes back with rustling shade
And apple-blossoms fill the air –
I have a rendezvous with Death
When Springs brings back blue days and fair.

It may be he shall take my hand
And lead me into his dark land
And close my eyes and quench my breath –
It may be I shall pass him still.
I have a rendezvous with Death
On some scarred slope of battered hill,
When Spring comes round again this year
And the first meadow-flowers appear.

God knows 'twere better to be deep
Pillowed in silk and scented down,
Where Love throbs out in blissful sleep
Pulse nigh to pulse, and breath to breath,
Where hushed awakenings are dear . . .
But I've a rendezvous with Death
At midnight in some flaming town,
When Spring trips north again this year,
And I to my pledged word am true.
I shall not fail that rendezvous.

Champagne, 1914–15

In the glad revels, in the happy fêtes,
    When cheeks are flushed, and glasses gilt and
      pearled
With the sweet wine of France that concentrates
    The sunshine and the beauty of the world,

Drink sometimes, you whose footsteps yet may tread
    The undisturbed, delightful paths of Earth,
To those whose blood, in pious duty shed,
    Hallows the soil where that same wine had birth.

Here, by devoted comrades laid away,
    Along our lines they slumber where they fell,
Beside the crater at the Ferme d'Alger
    And up the bloody slopes of La Pompelle,

And round the city whose cathedral towers
    The enemies of Beauty dared profane,
And in the mat of multicoloured flowers
    That clothe the sunny chalk-fields of Champagne

Under the little crosses where they rise
    The soldier rests. Now round him undismayed
The cannon thunders, and at night he lies
    At peace beneath the eternal fusillade . . .

That other generations might possess –
    From shame and menace free in years to come –
A richer heritage of happiness,
    He marched to that heroic martyrdom,

Esteeming less the forfeit that he paid
    Than undishonoured that his flag might float
Over the towers of liberty, he made
    His breast the bulwark and his blood the moat.

Obscurely sacrificed, his nameless tomb,
  Bare of the sculptor's art, the poet's lines,
Summer shall flush with poppy-fields in bloom,
  And Autumn yellow with maturing vines

There the grape-pickers at their harvesting
  Shall lightly tread and load their wicker trays,
Blessing his memory as they toil and sing
  In the slant sunshine of October days . . .

I love to think that if my blood should be
  So privileged to sink where his has sunk,
I shall not pass from Earth entirely,
  But when the banquet rings, when healths are
    drunk,

And faces that the joys of living fill
  Glow radiant with laughter and good cheer,
In beaming cups some spark of me shall still
  Brim toward the lips that once I held so dear.

So shall one coveting no higher plane
  Than nature clothes in colour and flesh and tone,
Even from the grave put upward to attain
  The dreams youth cherished and missed and might
    have known:

And that strong need that strove unsatisfied
  Toward earthly beauty in all forms it wore,
Not death itself shall utterly divide
  From the belovèd shapes it thirsted for.

Alas, how many an adept for whose arms
  Life held delicious offerings perished here,
How many in the prime of all that charms,
  Crowned with all gifts that conquer and endear!

Honour them not so much with tears and flowers,
  But you with whom the sweet fulfilment lies,
Where in the anguish of atrocious hours
  Turned their last thoughts and closed their dying
  eyes,

Rather when music on bright gatherings lays
  Its tender spell, and joy is uppermost,
Be mindful of the men they were, and raise
  Your glasses to them in one silent toast.

Drink to them – amorous of dear Earth as well,
  They asked no tribute lovelier than this –
And in the wine that ripened where they fell,
  Oh, frame your lips as though it were a kiss.

P. H. SHAW-STEWART
1888–1917
Killed, Cambrai, 30th December

I saw a man this morning

I saw a man this morning
Who did not wish to die:
I ask, and cannot answer,
If otherwise wish I.

Fair broke the day this morning
Against the Dardanelles;
The breeze blew soft, the morn's cheeks
Were cold as cold sea-shells.

But other shells are waiting
Across the Aegean sea,
Shrapnel and high explosive,
Shells and hells for me.

O hell of ships and cities,
Hell of men like me,
Fatal second Helen,
Why must I follow thee?

Achilles came to Troyland
And I to Chersonese:
He turned from wrath to battle,
And I from three days' peace.

Was it so hard, Achilles,
So very hard to die?
Thou knowest and I know not –
So much the happier I.

I will go back this morning
From Imbros over the sea;
Stand in the trench, Achilles,
Flame-capped, and shout for me.

G. B. SMITH

1894–1916
Died of wounds, Arras, 3rd December

April 1916

Now spring is come upon the hills in France,
And all the trees are delicately fair,
As heeding not the great guns' voice, by chance
Brought down the valley on a wandering air:
Now day by day upon the uplands bare
Do gentle, toiling horses draw the plough,
And birds sing often in the orchards where
Spring wantons it with blossoms on her brow –
Aye! but there is no peace in England now.

O little isle amid unquiet seas,
Though grisly messengers knock on many doors,
Though there be many storms among your trees
And all your banners rent with ancient wars;
Yet such a grace and majesty are yours
There be still some, whose glad heart suffereth
All hate can bring from her misgotten stores,
Telling themselves, so England's self draw breath,
That's all the happiness on this side of death.

CHARLES HAMILTON SORLEY

1895–1915
Killed, Loos, 13th October

When you see millions of the mouthless dead

When you see millions of the mouthless dead
Across your dreams in pale battalions go,
Say not soft things as other men have said,
That you'll remember. For you need not so.
Give them not praise. For, deaf, how should they know
It is not curses heaped on each gashed head?
Nor tears. Their blind eyes see not your tears flow.
Nor honour. It is easy to be dead.
Say only this, 'They are dead.' Then add thereto,

'Yet many a better one has died before.'
Then, scanning all the o'ercrowded mass, should you
Perceive one face that you loved heretofore,
It is a spook. None wears the face you knew.
Great death has made all his for evermore.

All the hills and vales along

All the hills and vales along
Earth is bursting into song,
And the singers are the chaps
Who are going to die perhaps.
      O sing, marching men,
      Till the valleys ring again.
      Give your gladness to earth's keeping,
      So be glad, when you are sleeping.

Cast away regret and rue,
Think what you are marching to,
Little give, great pass.
Jesus Christ and Barabbas
Were found the same day.
This died, that, went his way.
    So sing with joyful breath.
    For why, you are going to death.
    Teeming earth will surely store
    All the gladness that you pour.

Earth that never doubts nor fears
Earth that knows of death, not tears,
Earth that bore with joyful ease
Hemlock for Socrates,
Earth that blossomed and was glad
'Neath the cross that Christ had,
Shall rejoice and blossom too
When the bullet reaches you.
    Wherefore, men marching
    On the road to death, sing!
    Pour gladness on earth's head,
    So be merry, so be dead.

From the hills and valleys earth
Shouts back the sound of mirth,
Tramp of feet and lilt of song
Ringing all the road along.
All the music of their going,
Ringing swinging glad song-throwing,
Earth will echo still, when foot
Lies numb and voice mute.
    On marching men, on
    To the gates of death with song.
    Sow your gladness for earth's reaping,
    So you may be glad though sleeping.
    Strew your gladness on earth's bed,
    So be merry, so be dead.

J. E. STEWART
1889–1918
Killed, Ypres, 26th April

On Revisiting the Somme

If I were but a Journalist,
And had a heading every day
In double-column caps, I wist
I, too, could make it pay;

But still for me the shadow lies
Of tragedy. I cannot write
Of these so many Calvaries
As of a pageant fight;

For dead men look me through and through
With their blind eyes, and mutely cry
My name, as I were one they knew
In that red-rimmed July;

Others on new sensation bent
Will wander here, with some glib guide
Insufferably eloquent
Of secrets we would hide –

Hide in this battered crumbling line
Hide in these promiscuous graves,
Till one shall make our story shine
In the fierce light it craves.

J. W. STREETS

1885–1916
Killed, the Somme, 1st July

Serenity

Peace can be found in strife: artillery
Are belching forth this sweet, entrancing morn
Their projectiles of death: yet as in scorn,
Lost in the sky's clear, blue serenity
The larks in music sing their love new-born,
Trilling its joy, its natural ecstasy;
The butterfly along Life's drift is borne;
And seeking nectar drones the wand'ring bee.

Thus Nature is serene amid the strife:
And in the hearts of those who calmly stand
Here in the trenches ('mid Death's hail) un-mann'd,
Flinging at Death the treasure of a Life –
There is a peace unknown to those (deny!)
Who have not dared for Liberty to die.

EDWARD THOMAS
1878–1917
Killed, Arras, 9th April

Man and Dog

' 'Twill take some getting.' 'Sir, I think 'twill so.'
The old man stared up at the mistletoe
That hung too high in the poplar's crest for plunder
Of any climber, though not for kissing under:
Then he went on against the north-east wind –
Straight but lame, leaning on a staff new-skinned,
Carrying a brolly, flag-basket, and old coat, –
Towards Alton, ten miles off. And he had not
Done less from Chilgrove where he pulled up docks.
'Twere best, if he had had 'a money-box',
To have waited there till the sheep cleared a field
For what a half-week's flint-picking would yield.
His mind was running on the work he had done
Since he left Christchurch in the New Forest, one
Spring in the 'seventies, – navvying on dock and line
From Southampton to Newcastle-on-Tyne, –
In 'seventy-four a year of soldiering
With the Berkshires, – hoeing and harvesting
In half the shires where corn and couch will grow.
His sons, three sons, were fighting, but the hoe
And reap-hook he liked, or anything to do with trees.
He fell once from a poplar tall as these:
The Flying Man they called him in hospital.
'If I flew now, to another world I'd fall.'
He laughed and whistled to the small brown bitch
With spots of blue that hunted in the ditch.
Her foxy Welsh grandfather must have paired
Beneath him. He kept sheep in Wales and scared
Strangers, I will warrant, with his pearl eye
And trick of shrinking off as he were shy,

Then following close in silence for – for what?
'No rabbit, never fear, she ever got,
Yet always hunts. Today she nearly had one:
She would and she wouldn't. 'Twas like that. The bad
     one!
She's not much use, but still she's company,
Though I'm not. She goes everywhere with me.
So Alton I must reach tonight somehow:
I'll get no shakedown with that bedfellow
From farmers. Many a man sleeps worse tonight
Than I shall.' 'In the trenches.' 'Yes, that's right.
But they'll be out of that – I hope they be –
This weather, marching after the enemy.'
'And so I hope. Good luck.' And there I nodded
'Good-night. You keep straight on.' Stiffly he plodded;
And at his heels the crisp leaves scurried fast,
And the leaf-coloured robin watched. They passed,
The robin till next day, the man for good,
Together in the twilight of the wood.

The Owl

Downhill I came, hungry, and yet not starved;
Cold, yet had heat within me that was proof
Against the North wind; tired, yet so that rest
Had seemed the sweetest thing under a roof.

Then at the inn I had food, fire, and rest,
Knowing how hungry, cold, and tired was I.
All of the night was quite barred out except
An owl's cry, a most melancholy cry

Shaken out long and clear upon the hill,
No merry note, nor cause of merriment,
But one telling me plain what I escaped
And others could not, that night, as in I went.

And salted was my food, and my repose,
Salted and sobered, too, by the bird's voice
Speaking for all who lay under the stars,
Soldiers and poor, unable to rejoice.

In Memoriam (Easter, 1915)

The flowers left thick at nightfall in the wood
This Eastertide call into mind the men,
Now far from home, who, with their sweethearts, should
Have gathered them and will do never again.

Fifty Faggots

There they stand, on their ends, the fifty faggots
That once were underwood of hazel and ash
In Jenny Pinks's Copse. Now, by the hedge
Close packed, they make a thicket fancy alone
Can creep through with the mouse and wren. Next Spring
A blackbird or a robin will nest there,
Accustomed to them, thinking they will remain
Whatever is for ever to a bird:
This Spring it is too late; the swift has come.
'Twas a hot day for carrying them up:
Better they will never warm me, though they must
Light several Winters' fires. Before they are done
The war will have ended, many other things
Have ended, maybe, that I can no more
Foresee or more control than robin and wren.

This is no case of petty right or wrong

This is no case of petty right or wrong
That politicians or philosophers
Can judge. I hate not Germans, nor grow hot
With love of Englishmen, to please newspapers.
Beside my hate for one fat patriot
My hatred of the Kaiser is love true:–
A kind of god he is, banging a gong.
But I have not to choose between the two,
Or between justice and injustice. Dinned
With war and argument I read no more
Than in the storm smoking along the wind
Athwart the wood. Two witches' cauldrons roar.
From one the weather shall rise clear and gay;
Out of the other an England beautiful
And like her mother that died yesterday.
Little I know or care if, being dull,
I shall miss something that historians
Can rake out of the ashes when perchance
The phoenix broods serene above their ken.
But with the best and meanest Englishmen
I am one in crying, God save England, lest
We lose what never slaves and cattle blessed.
The ages made her that made us from dust:
She is all we know and live by, and we trust
She is good and must endure, loving her so:
And as we love ourselves we hate her foe.

Rain

Rain, midnight rain, nothing but the wild rain
On this bleak hut, and solitude, and me
Remembering again that I shall die
And neither hear the rain nor give it thanks
For washing me cleaner than I have been
Since I was born into this solitude.
Blessed are the dead that the rain rains upon:
But here I pray that none whom once I loved
Is dying tonight or lying still awake
Solitary, listening to the rain,
Either in pain or thus in sympathy
Helpless among the living and the dead,
Like a cold water among broken reeds,
Myriads of broken reeds all still and stiff,
Like me who have no love which this wild rain
Has not dissolved except the love of death,
If love it be for what is perfect and
Cannot, the tempest tells me, disappoint.

Roads

I love roads:
The goddesses that dwell
Far along invisible
are my favourite gods.

Roads go on
While we forget, and are
Forgotten like a star
That shoots and is gone.

On this earth 'tis sure
We men have not made
Anything that doth fade
So soon, so long endure:

The hill road wet with rain
In the sun would not gleam
Like a winding stream
If we trod it not again.

They are lonely
While we sleep, lonelier
For lack of the traveller
Who is now a dream only.

From dawn's twilight
And all the clouds like sheep
On the mountains of sleep
They wind into the night.

The next turn may reveal
Heaven: upon the crest
The close pine clump, at rest
And black, may Hell conceal.

Often footsore, never
Yet of the road I weary,
Though long and steep and dreary,
As it winds on for ever.

Helen of the roads,
The mountain ways of Wales
And the Mabinogion tales
Is one of the true gods,

Abiding in the trees,
The threes and fours so wise,
The larger companies,
That by the roadside be,

And beneath the rafter
Else uninhabited
Excepting by the dead;
And it is her laughter

At morn and night I hear
When the thrush cock sings
Bright irrelevant things,
And when the chanticleer

Calls back to their own night
Troops that make loneliness
With their light footsteps' press,
As Helen's own are light.

Now all roads lead to France
And heavy is the tread
Of the living; but the dead
Returning lightly dance:

Whatever the road bring
To me or take from me,
They keep me company
With their pattering,

Crowding the solitude
Of the loops over the downs,
Hushing the roar of towns
And their brief multitude.

February Afternoon

Men heard this roar of parleying starlings, saw,
    A thousand years ago even as now,
    Black rooks with white gulls following the plough
So that the first are last until a caw
Commands that last are first again, – a law
    Which was of old when one, like me, dreamed how
    A thousand years might dust lie on his brow
Yet thus would birds do between hedge and shaw.

Time swims before me, making as a day
    A thousand years, while the broad ploughland oak
    Roars mill-like and men strike and bear the stroke
    Of war as ever, audacious or resigned,
And God still sits aloft in the array
    That we have wrought him, stone-deaf and stone-blind.

The Cherry Trees

The cherry trees bend over and are shedding,
On the old road where all that passed are dead,
Their petals, strewing the grass as for a wedding
This early May morn when there is none to wed.

As the Team's Head-Brass

As the team's head-brass flashed out on the turn
The lovers disappeared into the wood.
I sat among the boughs of the fallen elm
That strewed the angle of the fallow, and
Watched the plough narrowing a yellow square
Of charlock. Every time the horses turned
Instead of treading me down, the ploughman leaned
Upon the handles to say or ask a word,
About the weather, next about the war.
Scraping the share he faced towards the wood,
And screwed along the furrow till the brass flashed
Once more.
          The blizzard felled the elm whose crest
I sat in, by a woodpecker's round hole,
The ploughman said, 'When will they take it away?'
'When the war's over.' So the talk began –
One minute and an interval of ten,
A minute more and the same interval.
'Have you been out?' 'No.' 'And don't want to, perhaps?'
'If I could only come back again, I should.
I could spare an arm. I shouldn't want to lose
A leg. If I should lose my head, why, so,
I should want nothing more . . . Have many gone
From here?' 'Yes.' 'Many lost?' 'Yes, a good few.
Only two teams work on the farm this year.
One of my mates is dead. The second day
In France they killed him. It was back in March,
The very night of the blizzard, too. Now if
He had stayed here we should have moved the tree.'
'And I should not have sat here. Everything
Would have been different. For it would have been
Another world.' 'Ay, and a better, though
If we could see all all might seem good.' Then
The lovers came out of the wood again:
The horses started and for the last time
I watched the clods crumble and topple over
After the ploughshare and the stumbling team.

Gone, gone again

Gone, gone again,
May, June, July,
And August gone,
Again gone by,

Not memorable
Save that I saw them go,
As past the empty quays
The rivers flow.

And now again,
In the harvest rain,
The Blenheim oranges
Fall grubby from the trees

As when I was young –
And when the lost one was here –
And when the war began
To turn young men to dung.

Look at the old house,
Outmoded, dignified,
Dark and untenanted,
With grass growing instead

Of the footsteps of life,
The friendliness, the strife;
In its beds have lain
Youth, love, age, and pain:

I am something like that;
Only I am not dead,
Still breathing and interested
In the house that is not dark:–

I am something like that:
Not one pane to reflect the sun,
For the schoolboys to throw at –
They have broken every one.

A Private

This ploughman dead in battle slept out of doors
Many a frozen night, and merrily
Answered staid drinkers, good bedmen, and all bores:
'At Mrs Greenland's Hawthorn Bush', said he,
'I slept.' None knew which bush. Above the town,
Beyond 'The Drover', a hundred spot the down
In Wiltshire. And where now at last he sleeps
More sound in France – that, too, he secret keeps.

A. G. WEST

1891–1917
Killed, the Somme, 3rd April

The Night Patrol

France, March 1916

Over the top! The wire's thin here, unbarbed
Plain rusty coils, not staked, and low enough:
Full of old tins, though – 'When you're through, all three,
Aim quarter left for fifty yards or so,
Then straight for that new piece of German wire;
See if it's thick, and listen for a while
For sounds of working; don't run any risks;
About an hour; now, over!'
                                And we placed
Our hands on the topmost sand-bags, leapt, and stood
A second with curved backs, then crept to the wire,
Wormed ourselves tinkling through, glanced back, and
    dropped.
The sodden ground was splashed with shallow pools,
And tufts of crackling cornstalks, two years old,
No man had reaped, and patches of spring grass.
Half-seen, as rose and sank the flares, were strewn
With the wrecks of our attack: the bandoliers.
Packs rifles, bayonets, belts, and haversacks,
Shell fragments, and the huge whole forms of shells
Shot fruitlessly – and everywhere the dead.
Only the dead were always present – present
As a vile sickly smell of rottenness;
The rustling stubble and the early grass,
The slimy pools – the dead men stank through all,
Pungent and sharp: as bodies loomed before,

And as we passed they stank: then dulled away
To what vague foetor, all encompassing,

Infecting earth and air. They lay, all clothed,
Each in some new and piteous attitude
That we well marked to guide us back: as he,
Outside our wire, that lay on his back and crossed
His legs Crusader-wise; I smiled at that,
And thought on Elia and his Temple Church.
From him, at quarter-left, lay a small corpse,
Down in a hollow, huddled as in bed,
That one of us put his hand on unawares.
Next was a bunch of half a dozen men
All blown to bits, an archipelago
Of corrupt fragments, vexing to us three,
Who had no light to see by, save the flares.
On such a trail, so lit, for ninety yards

We crawled on belly and elbows, till we saw,
Instead of lumpish dead before our eyes,
The stakes and crosslines of the German wire.
We lay in shelter of the last dead man,
Ourselves as dead, and heard their shovels ring
Turning the earth, then talk and cough at times.
A sentry fired and a machine-gun spat;
They shot a flare above us, when it fell
And spluttered out in the pools of No Man's Land,
We turned and crawled past the remembered dead:
Past him and him, and them and him, until,
For he lay some way apart, we caught the scent
Of the Crusader and slid past his legs,
And through the wire and home, and got our rum.

God! How I hate you, you young cheerful men

God! How I hate you, you young cheerful men,
Whose pious poetry blossoms on your graves
As soon as you are in them, nurtured up
By the salt of your corruption, and the tears
Of mothers, local vicars, college deans,
And flanked by prefaces and photographs
From all your minor poet friends – the fools –
Who paint their sentimental elegies
Where sure, no angel treads; and, living, share
The dead's brief immortality.
       Oh Christ!
To think that one could spread the ductile wax
Of his fluid youth to Oxford's glowing fires
And take her seal so ill! Hark how one chants –
'Oh happy to have lived these epic days' –
'These epic days!' And he'd been to France,
And seen the trenches, glimpsed the huddled dead
In the periscope, hung in the rusting wire:
Choked by their sickly foetor, day and night
Blown down his throat: stumbled through ruined hearths,
Proved all that muddy brown monotony,
Where blood's the only coloured thing. Perhaps
Had seen a man killed, a sentry shot at night,
Hunched as he fell, his feet on the firing-step,
His neck against the back slope of the trench,
And the rest doubled up between, his head
Smashed like an egg-shell, and the warm grey brain
Spattered all bloody on the parados:
Had flashed a torch on his face, and known his friend,
Shot, breathing hardly, in ten minutes – gone!
Yet still God's in His heaven, all is right
In the best possible of worlds. The woe,
Even His scaled eyes must see, is partial, only
A seeming woe, we cannot understand.
God loves us, God looks down on this our strife
And smiles in pity, blows a pipe at times
And calls some warriors home. We do not die,

God would not let us, he is too 'intense',
Too 'passionate', a whole day sorrows He
Because a grass-blade dies. How rare life is!
On earth, the love and fellowship of men,
Men sternly banded: banded for what end?
Banded to maim and kill their fellow men –
For even Huns are men. In heaven above
A genial umpire, a good judge of sport,
Won't let us hurt each other! Let's rejoice
God keeps us faithful, pens us still in fold.
Ah, what a faith is ours (almost, it seems,
Large, as a mustard-seed) – we trust and trust,
Nothing can shake us! Ah, how good God is
To suffer us be born just now, when youth
That else would rust, can slake his blade in gore,
Where very God Himself does seem to walk
The bloody fields of Flanders He so loves!

T. P. CAMERON WILSON

1889–1918
Killed, the Somme, 23rd March

Magpies in Picardy

The magpies in Picardy
Are more than I can tell.
They flicker down the dusty roads
And cast a magic spell
On the men who march through Picardy,
Through Picardy to Hell.

(The blackbird flies with panic,
The swallow goes like light,
The finches move like ladies,
The owl floats by at night;
But the great and flashing magpie
He flies as artists might.)

A magpie in Picardy
Told me secret things –
Of the music in white feathers,
And the sunlight that sings
And dances in deep shadows –
He told me with his wings.

(The hawk is cruel and rigid,
He watches from a height;
The rook is slow and sombre,
The robin loves to fight;
But the great and flashing magpie
He flies as lovers might.)

He told me that in Picardy,
An age ago or more,
While all his fathers still were eggs,
These dusty highways bore

Brown singing soldiers marching out
Through Picardy to war.

He said that still through chaos
Works on the ancient plan
And two things have altered not
Since first the world began –
The beauty of the wild green earth
And the bravery of man.

(For the sparrow flies unthinking
And quarrels in his flight;
The heron trails his legs behind,
The lark goes out of sight;
But the great and flashing magpie
He flies as poets might.)

W. B. YEATS
1865–1939

An Irish Airman Foresees His Death

I know that I shall meet my fate
Somewhere among the clouds above;
Those that I fight I do not hate,
Those that I guard I do not love;
My country is Kiltartan Cross,
My countrymen Kiltartan's poor,
No likely end could bring them loss
Or leave them happier than before.
Nor law, nor duty bade me fight,
Nor public men, nor cheering crowds,
A lonely impulse of delight
Drove to this tumult in the clouds;
I balanced all, brought all to mind,
The years to come seemed waste of breath,
A waste of breath the years behind
In balance with this life, this death.

On Being Asked for a War Poem

I think it better that in times like these
A poet's mouth be silent, for in truth
We have no gift to set a statesman right;
He has had enough of meddling who can please
A young girl in the indolence of her youth,
Or an old man upon a winter's night.

INDEX OF POEM TITLES

INDEX OF FIRST LINES

The Wordsworth Poetry Library

Works of

Matthew Arnold

William Blake

The Brontë Sisters

Rupert Brooke

Robert Browning

Elizabeth Barrett Browning

Robert Burns

Lord Byron

Geoffrey Chaucer

G. K. Chesterton

John Clare

Samuel Taylor Coleridge

Emily Dickinson

John Donne

John Dryden

Thomas Hardy

George Herbert

Gerard Manley Hopkins

A. E. Housman

James Joyce

John Keats

Rudyard Kipling

D. H. Lawrence

Henry Wadsworth Longfellow

Macaulay

Andrew Marvell

John Milton

Wilfred Owen

'Banjo' Paterson

Edgar Allen Poe

Alexander Pope

John Wilmot, Earl of Rochester

Christina Rossetti

Sir Walter Scott

William Shakespeare

P. B. Shelley

Edmund Spenser

Algernon Swinburne

Alfred Lord Tennyson

Edward Thomas

Walt Whitman

Oscar Wilde

William Wordsworth

W. B. Yeats

Anthologies & Collections

Restoration and
Eighteenth-Century Verse

Nineteenth-Century Verse

The Wordsworth Book of
First World War Poetry

Love Poems

The Metaphysical Poets

The Wordsworth Book of Sonnets